BRETHREN IN CHIVALRY

BRETHREN IN CHIVALRY

A Celebration of the Two Hundred Years
of the
Great Priory of the United Religious, Military and Masonic
Orders of the Temple and of St John of Jerusalem, Palestine,
Rhodes and Malta of England and Wales and Provinces Overseas
1791 – 1991

FREDERICK SMYTH

The royalties on this book are to be devoted to the Ophthalmic Hospital of the Order of St John at Jerusalem

First published 1991
This facsimile reprint 2017

ISBN 978 0 85318 552 9

Published by Lewis Masonic

an imprint of Ian Allan Publishing Ltd, Addlestone, Surrey KT15 2SF.
Printed in England.

Visit the Lewis Masonic website at www.lewismasonic.co.uk

Picture Credits
Every effort has been made to identify and correctly attribute photographic credits. Should any error have occurred this is entirely unintentional.

British Library Cataloguing in Publication Data

Smyth, Frederick
Brethren in Chivalry: a celebration of the United Religious, Military and Masonic Orders of the Temple and of St John of Jreusalem, Palestine, Rhodes and Malta of England and Walesm 1771-1991
1. England. Freemasonry, history
I. Title
366.10942

CONTENTS

APPENDICES

ILLUSTRATIONS

ACKNOWLEDGEMENTS

My first words of gratitude must be to the Most Eminent and Supreme Grand Master for entrusting to me the writing of this bicentenary volume and for writing the Foreword to it. For much of the research, the Great Vice-Chancellor and his colleagues gave me ready access to the archives at Mark Masons' Hall and patiently submitted to questioning.

Tribute must be paid in no small measure to the work of G. E. W. Bridge. His unselfish industry some years ago, as the librarian at Mark Masons' Hall, provided for future students an enormous quantity of carefully classified material on all the degrees and Orders beyond the Craft and Royal Arch. Without it this book could not have seen the light. One of his successors, R. M. Handfield-Jones, produced in 1973 a booklet about the United Orders and this too has been most helpful.

From a lengthy list of those who have offered or have been asked for advice and information, to all of whom my thanks are due, I must mention in particular M.E. and S. Knight Norman A. Pellow (Grand Master of Ireland), R.E.Fr. Rex N. Lewis (Grand Secretary of Scotland), Peter Lowick (the Grand Superintendent of the Camp of Baldwyn), Colonel Ewen McEwen, Dennis Thomas, Jack Dribbell, Brian Chappell, Jean Heineman and the late Sinclair Bruce. John Hamill, Librarian and Curator at Freemasons' Hall, kindly produced several of the illustrations for this book and acknowledgement is given therefor to the Board of General Purposes.

To my wife, whose exemplary patience allowed me to spend even more time than usual at my desk, my heartfelt thanks are due.

The abbreviation *AQC*, used throughout the text, stands for *Ars Quatuor Coronatorum*, the annual transactions of Quatuor Coronati Lodge No 2076.

HAROLD DEVEREUX STILL, C.St.J., G.C.T.
Most Eminent and Supreme Grand Master Great Priory of England, etc.
(D J Photographers, Swansea)

FOREWORD

by the Most Eminent and Supreme Grand Master,
Harold Devereux Still, C.St.J., G.C.T.

All the members of our United Orders will have a deep sense of gratitude to Eminent Knight Major F. H. Smyth, Past Great Herald, for the diligent research and devoted application which he has undertaken in the preparation of this book. It is clear, concise, eminently readable, and fills a long-felt need.

I am sure that all those who seek a more erudite history of our Orders will appreciate how well E. Kt. Smyth traces the development of our present-day objects and precepts from the spirit which guided the Medieval Knights.

It is my hope that copies of this excellent text may be available in all our Provinces and Preceptories for the benefit of all Knights as a standard book of reference.

INTRODUCTION

ALTHOUGH WE ARE in no doubt at all that we are quite correctly celebrating, in the year 1991, the bicentenary of our Great Priory, we have to admit to some difficulty in settling upon a date on which the celebrations could most appropriately take place. In our *Liber Ordinis Templi* there is an excellent list of those who have ruled over us and from this we can see that Thomas Dunckerley is regarded as having assumed the functions of Grand Master in February 1791, although he was not installed as such until 24 June. There was plenty of activity in the intervening period, as a later chapter will tell us.

1791, therefore, is the year in which a governing organization for our Orders came into being. With the exception of the Craft (1717) and the Royal Arch (1766) — and to them in several senses we owe our existence — we are the longest-established masonic authority in England. It can be claimed of various degrees and Orders that they were being *worked* at early dates but it was not until the 19th century that a Supreme Council for the Ancient and Accepted Rite (1845), a Grand Mark Lodge (1856) and several other sovereign hierarchies were established.

In taking stock, so to speak, of the past two centuries we cannot do so in splendid isolation. Much of our early history is interwoven with that of our sister Great Priories of Ireland and Scotland; a great deal of what we shall be writing of our more recent years affects, or is affected by, what has happened in other countries. This book has therefore something of an international flavour and it is hoped that it will thus be of interest to our brother knights 'wheresoe'er dispersed', but that they will understand and forgive the inevitable absence from this text of much that is familiar in their annals.

Because of our links, however tenuous, with the military knights of the Middle Ages it is right that we should recall something of their story and trace it forward so far as can properly be done. We can then consider how and when the masonic thread weaves itself into the tapestry and allow it to lead us to the point where our two centuries begin.

1

THE MEDIEVAL KNIGHTHOODS

OUR UNITED MASONIC orders of today can claim to have inherited little more than the names of the two knightly fraternities which were formed and developed in the Holy Land during the first and second Crusades. Even so, it seems right to preface the tale of *our* two centuries with accounts of the Hospitallers and Templars of the Middle Ages. Their many chroniclers are so much in agreement that it is has been a relatively simple task to distil from their writings the necessarily brief records which follow.

THE HOSPITALLERS

The Earliest Years

It has been said that 'the history of the Order can be traced back so far that it is difficult to name an exact date for its beginning' (E. D. Renwick, *A Short History of the Order of St. John,* 6th ed, 1971, page 7). Certainly, a hostel in Jerusalem for pilgrims to the holy places of Christianity was established in about AD 600, at the instigation of Pope Gregory I, and this survived for many years the Muslim occupation of the country.

Early in the ninth century, Charlemagne, King of the Franks (768-814), was permitted by the Caliph Haroun-al-Raschid to rebuild and extend the hostel but some two centuries later a persecution of the Christians led to its destruction and that of the Church of the Holy Sepulchre. The necessary continuance of trade, nevertheless, gave to merchants from Amalfi – a small republic in what we now know as Italy – the opportunity of purchasing the site of Charlemagne's buildings and they erected both a new church and a hospital for Christian pilgrims. The insignia of Amalfi was the eight-pointed white cross, and this was chosen by the Benedictines, to whom the care of the hospital had been assigned, as their emblem. It has ever since distinguished the Orders and fraternities which have been predicated upon the foundation at Jerusalem. Sadly, the varying attitudes of the Muslim overlords and their military forces seldom left the pilgrims at peace and the holy places became virtually inaccessible. The frustrations which this engendered for Christians in Europe led, in 1095, to an appeal from Pope Urban II for action and the energetic preaching of Peter the Hermit inspired the first of the Crusades. In 1099 the Christian army reached Jerusalem and seized the city.

During the Crusades

The Warden of the hospital at that time was Gerard of Martigues and, with encouragement from Godfrey of Bouillon – by election the ruler of Jerusalem – and assisted by gifts from him and from many of the Crusaders, it was possible for Gerard to reorganize the hospital and found an Order of Hospitallers. The brethren of this Order, under monastic vows of poverty, chastity and obedience, changed their rule from that of the Benedictines to the less restrictive regime of the Augustinians and adopted a black habit, on its breast the Amalfi cross.

Among the buildings with which the Order was endowed during this period was a monastery which had been dedicated to John the Baptist by the Greek Church and he was chosen as the patron saint of the Hospitallers. Pope Paschal II in 1113 formally recognized the Order and gave them the right to elect a Master. Gerard continued as their head until his death in 1118.

His successor, Raymond Dupuy, recast the organization in a military mould, with three classes of membership: knights to defend Jerusalem against the Saracens, chaplains to continue the religious traditions and serving brethren to discharge more lowly functions. Unlike the Templars, who were by now establishing themselves, the Hospitallers never became a wholly military Order, although their knights were ready to fight side by side with those of the Temple. Their care for the sick and needy continued and, when they were later forced to move to other places, the establishment of a local hospital was always given priority.

Expansion

By now, they had been given land and lordships in western Europe and certain knights were appointed as Preceptors to administer these possessions, and they founded convents or commanderies of the Order within which to function.

At Jerusalem, as their numbers grew, fellow-countrymen among the Hospitallers grouped themselves in relation to their native languages and so developed the seven *langues* (tongues) which were to be an important characteristic: of Provence, Auvergne, France, Italy, Spain, England and Germany.

Dress

It is of interest to the masonic knights of today that, over their chain mail or armour, the military brethren wore a red tunic faced with a plain white cross, while in the convent the black mantle with the Amalfi cross was assumed. The candidate for admission to the Order was informed that the four arms of the cross were symbolic of the cardinal virtues – prudence, fortitude, temperance and justice – and that the eight points represented the beatitudes which issue therefrom.

The Later Crusades

We cannot here pursue in any detail the story of the Holy Land through the later Crusades. The second, of 1147, had been preached by Bernard of Clairvaux; the third, of 1189, was of particular note to Englishmen because for it Richard the Lionheart joined Frederick Barbarossa of Germany and Philip of France. Some diversity of opinion confuses the fourth Crusade, which earned little credit; within some unworthy bargaining for Venetian sea-transport, the European Christian armies found themselves diverted to attack Constantinople and the Byzantine Christians, virtually as mercenaries of Venice. From this expedition developed the rift between the Churches of the East and West which has never been entirely healed.

Still more confusion arises on the subject of these further Crusades; some writers describe four more while others end the series with the seventh. It is, however, generally agreed that the last of these – whether styled the seventh or the eighth – was organized by Louis of France in 1270, and that Edward of England, later King Edward I, joined him at the head of the armies.

During these long years of strife, often exacerbated by quarrels among the royal leaders but intermittently relieved by truces, the Hospitallers and Templars suffered greatly. No fewer than 230 of them were executed at Saladin's orders when they refused to renounce their faith when captured. The Saracens having won Jerusalem in 1187, the Hospitallers began what was to be an extended series of moves, firstly to Margat (Marqab) in what we now know as Syria and then, after ten years, south to Acre where their hospital earned high praise. The wars, meanwhile, dragged on and great numbers of the knights died in battle. In 1291 the Saracens began their siege of Acre, where the defenders included about 240 Templars and 140 Hospitallers. Despite a brave defence against overwhelming odds, the Christian cause was lost and only the seriously-wounded Master, John de Villiers, and six other Knights Hospitaller survived to be carried from the Holy Land.

To Cyprus and Rhodes

They first moved to Cyprus, where the Master established a convent at Limassol. The Order already owned the neighbouring castle of Colossis; this still stands and the British Order of St. John helps to maintain it. Knights were called from Europe to a meeting of the Chapter-General and it was determined that nothing should prevent the work for which the Hospitallers had been brought into being – the service of the sick and care for pilgrims. A naval role was now found for the knights and galleys were acquired so that pilgrims *en route* to the Holy Land could be defended against the pirates who infested the Mediterranean. Thus was assumed, to some extent, a duty for which the Templars had been established.

When, after only nineteen years in Cyprus, it became impossible to remain there, Rhodes – with its excellent harbours – proved an ideal location from which to continue to operate and here the Order had its headquarters for more than two centuries. There is a fascinating story to be told (but not in this book) of the Hospitallers during this period, which leads from the Middle Ages into the sixteenth century. The events of 1522 in Rhodes, when again the aggressors were of the Muslim faith, are important to us and we shall describe them in chapter 2.

THE TEMPLARS

We have so far given pride of place and more extended treatment to the Hospitallers because they were already established as an Order in Jerusalem when a second fraternity of Christian knights developed within the forces of the Crusades. (A third, the Order of Teutonic Knights of St. Mary's Hospital, followed some years later in 1180. They too suffered much in the defence of the Holy Land.)

The Order of the Temple is Founded

In 1118 – some sources give 1119 – Hugues de Payens and Godfrey (or Geoffrey) de Saint Adhemar (several versions of these names are recorded) and seven other crusading knights bound themselves by vows, taken before the Patriarch of Jerusalem, of poverty, chastity and obedience and to defend the Christian kingdom over which Baldwin II now ruled. More especially they charged themselves with protecting pilgrims on their hazardous journey up to Jerusalem from the coast. The King granted them quarters on the site of King Solomon's Temple and they became known as 'The Poor Fellow-Soldiers of Christ and the Temple of Solomon'. Poverty was certainly exemplified in an early seal of the fraternity which depicted two knights mounted on one horse and that seal, of course, is now used by our masonic Order, surrounded by the Latin version of their early title: *Pauperes Commilitones Christi et Templi Salomonis*.

It took some years for the new Order to become established, but then both the Church and the kingdom took more interest. Fulk, Count of Anjou, a later King of Jerusalem, took vows with them; other candidates followed, property was acquired and a flow of gifts began.

The Order Expands

They had adopted a Benedictine rule but in 1126, at the prompting of Baldwin II, de Payens led a small party to Rome to seek advice. Pope Honorius II received them kindly but referred them to a Council of the Church to be held at Troyes in 1128. (This delay would not have been entirely unacceptable to de Payens for Troyes was in his homeland of Champagne.) The Council, clearly anticipating a great future for the Templars, delegated the devising of a new Constitution for them to Bernard of Clairvaux, a renowned Benedictine. Under this, the rule would be harsh and ascetic; luxury and display were to be avoided; wordly pleasures, even hunting, were to be forbidden. At first none but men of rank and station could be admitted but, as for the Hospitallers, the need for serving brethren was soon recognized.

Dress

From this Constitution also derived the white mantle which to this day distinguishes a Knight Templar. In 1147, the red cross – a symbol of martyrdom – was added to the garment. A white coif (from which our hood is derived) was worn upon the head; in the field a helmet was a necessary protection but a cap of red cloth replaced this within the convent.

Provinces are Established

De Payens, having obtained this revised rule, returned to Jerusalem by a most circuitous route, touring France, England and Scotland in his progress. Sovereigns and subjects endowed his Order with lands and it was – as had been the case with the older Order – necessary to set up local administrative centres. These were called preceptories and they served also as recruitment offices for the work in the Holy Land. The English province of the Templars (which comprehended Scotland and Ireland) was inaugurated by de Payens in 1128; other provinces included Portugal, Castile, Leon, Aragon, France, Aquitaine, Provence, Germany, Italy, Sicily and, in the eastern Mediterranean, Antioch and Tripoli.

Privileges were acquired: freedom from the jurisdiction of bishops, the Pope being the only superior; Templar houses were given the right of sanctuary and property was exempt from taxation and tithing.

The End of the Crusades

We must recall, as we proceed with an outline of their history, their struggle in company with the Hospitallers against the Saracens and the hardships which – in the Holy Land at least – they suffered for the Christian faith. One record claims that no fewer than 20,000 perished there.

After the fall of Acre to the Muslims, the remnants of the Templar Order moved to Cyprus, which it seems that they had earlier purchased from Richard I. They did not however remain, as had the Hospitallers, in the Mediterranean. The knights retired to the various preceptories in their native lands and enjoyed the quiet life.

Decline and Dissolution

Undoubtedly many of the Templars lost sight of the noble aims which had inspрired their predecessors. They were in time accused of arrogance, of licentiousness, of apostasy from their Christian faith, of treachery, of oppression, of extortion; many of the complaints against them were probably inspired only by envy of the wealth which they had progressively acquired by quite honest means and by their freedom from taxes and similar 'community charges'. We cannot here investigate their culpability or otherwise. As with the present-day strictures against Freemasonry, the detractors would have seized upon individual malpractices and visited them upon the Order as a whole.

There was, especially in France, relentless persecution of the Templars and this came to a head with the torture and death at the stake of Jacques de Molay, the Grand Master in 1314. In Spain, Portugal and Germany, on the other hand, the Order was adjudged innocent of the alleged offences, and in Britain the verdict seems to have been 'not proven'.

The Pope dissolved the Order and ruled that its possessions should be made over to the Hospitallers, who for a while made merry on their new-found wealth but then recovered themselves.

For some years, of course, individual Knights Templar survived. There are tales of preceptories which, still in existence, continued to admit novices; perhaps the strongest of the legends is centred upon Scotland where it is said that the papal decree of dissolution was never put into effect. It could be that there were amalgamations on a modest scale between surviving Templars and the Hospitallers. Something more will be said a little later about the 'Scottish connection', although the bait so temptingly offered in *The Temple and the Lodge* (Michael Baigent and Richard Leigh, 1989) must be refused because walking in the clouds is always dangerous!

There are those who believe in an unbroken succession of Grand Masters of the Order of the Temple from de Molay onwards and this we shall have something to say about in Appendix A, on the Charter of Larmenius.

In the Footsteps of the Templars

Given the time and the necessary finance, it would be possible to travel to the Holy Land and elsewhere overseas where the knights served and fought, and to see the remains of the fortifications which they so nobly defended. It is, however, rather more practical to ponder upon the traces, some quite considerable, of their possessions in England.

We are generally aware that the word 'Temple' in a place-name is likely to indicate that, in the Middle Ages, the Knights Templar had established themselves in the vicinity. Cressing Temple in Essex had a preceptory founded in 1136 and from it there survive two splendid barns. At Temple Balsall in Warwickshire, although the church is much altered, some of the knights' buildings are still to be seen, including a Great Hall, and are used by the Temple Balsall Preceptory No. 340 of our United Orders. And Temple – just that – in Cornwall on Bodmin Moor has but a few stones and the bowl of the font remaining from the Norman church built there by the Order, but is none the less worth a visit.

Those familiar with London's Temple Church and the circular form of its more ancient portion will associate that form with the medieval knights, sometimes because it has been thought to perpetuate the shape of a tent but probably more often for its assumed relevance to the Church of the Holy Sepulchre at Jerusalem. There are, or have been, quite a few other round or oval churches which were Templar foundations. That at Cambridge, which is perhaps – despite restorations – the most evocative, and that at Northampton are both dedicated to the Holy Sepulchre. It is said that the ruined chapel in Ludlow Castle was a Templar church but the evidence is not conclusive. The Temple Church at Bristol – also ruined, but by wartime bombs – was found after excavations to have had an oval form. The round church at Little Maplestead was one which was built by the Hospitallers who, of course, had taken over those of the Templars.

Certain churches and chapels of a more usual conformation are also of interest. At Dinsmore Manor in Herefordshire there was a commandery of the Hospitallers and its chapel accommodates an annual service of the Sir Thomas Docwra Preceptory No 376. The church at Down Ampney in Gloucestershire is another Hospitaller foundation. Lastly, the church at Sompting in Sussex – best-known for its unique 'Rhenish helm' tower – now includes as its south transept what was once a quite separate Templar chapel.

2

THE KNIGHTS OF MALTA

The Knights at Rhodes

IN CHAPTER 1 WE left the medieval[1] Hospitallers *en route* from Cyprus to Rhodes and we must now accompany them and bring their story up to date for, unlike the Templars, they were able — often with great difficulty — to continue to the present day.

In 1310 the knights captured the island of Rhodes and drove out the pirates who had long used it as a base. Thereafter, for over two centuries it became the centre of Christianity in the eastern part of the Mediterranean. Its galleys gave protection to the maritime traders between Europe and the East from those who had molested them. It was early in this stage of their history that the Hospitallers were given the possessions of the disbanded Templars but it took quite some time for them to be able to lay their hands on them, especially so in the case of estates and buildings.

There are in the masonic Order of Malta certain offices which existed among the knights at Rhodes and, no doubt, continued to exist: the Mareschal or Marshal, who controlled military operations; the Baillies or Bailiffs who headed the *langues* or tongues; the Hospitaller was concerned with the charitable aspects and, not surprisingly, with the hospital which was the central feature of the Order's headquarters; the Admiral was the Baillie of Italy; his colleague of England bore also the title of Turcopolier because he commanded the Turcopoles, the native mounted bowmen; the Commander, whom we take to be the forerunner of the Conservator, had the oversight of estates and properties.

The knights at Rhodes were also involved with naval action against the Turks, who had supplanted the Saracens as the leaders of the Muslim nations. Eventually the Turks became strong enough to take Constantinople, in 1453, and then they turned their attention to Rhodes. A massive attempt on the island fortress began in 1480 but failed. In 1522 they tried again and this time, after a prolonged siege, in which the Turks suffered enormous losses, the garrison — weakened by hunger and illness — surrendered on honourable terms. They left Rhodes in their own ships, with their belongings and sailed to Candia on the island of Crete.

The Knights at Malta

After a period of uncertainty, when the future of the Order was in some danger, the Holy Roman Emperor Charles V gave to the knights the island of Malta and to it they came in 1530, staying until they yielded it to Napoleon Bonaparte in 1798.

The more detailed story of the Knights of Malta during those 268 years is of the greatest interest but cannot be pursued here. In 1565, after an earlier half-hearted attack, the Turks laid siege to the island for several months and there was an heroic defence against enormous odds. Eventually, with the aid of a relieving force from Sicily, the enemy turned tail and for the next two centuries and more the knights were able to devote themselves to more peaceful pursuits, including the erection of *auberges* (inns) for their several *langues*, a palace for the Grand Master and a splendid hospital.

The duty of protecting sea trade continued, as did other naval and military functions, but eventually — as the calls for such services became fewer — there was a slackening of discipline and the Order in Malta could be seen to have outlived much of its original purpose. They maintained the hospital, of course, to a very high standard but many of the knights were able to enjoy their wealth in idleness. During the revolution which began in 1789 the properties in France of the three French *langues* were confiscated. The income from these had been a major source of funds for the Order in Malta and the shortfall hastened the decline. When Napoleon's fleet arrived off Valletta in 1798, little resistance was offered. The island and all that the knights owned therein were seized and portable property, which included a good deal of valuable plate, was taken to France, greatly to the financial benefit of the future Emperor.

The Knightly Freemasons

Desmond Caywood, in a paper, 'Freemasonry and the Knights of Malta' (*AQC* 83, 1970), drew attention to the fact that St John's Lodge of Secrecy and Harmony was warranted as No 539 under the premier Grand Lodge in 1789. The petition had been signed by several distinguished Knights Hospitaller or of St John. Caywood was able to include many details, such as the names, nationalities and rank in the Order of the members of the lodge. Catholic pressures caused the lodge to 'go underground' and its last report to London was in 1792. It could not have existed after 1798 and it was erased at the Union of the two Grand Lodges in 1813. Caywood had good reason to believe that it was not the only lodge to have existed in Malta in the days when the knights bore sway.

The Sovereign Order of Malta

Some of the knights, after the surrender, abandoned their vows and returned to their native countries. A few however went to Russia and were there given imperial protection, but soon struck out on their own, sojourning in various Italian towns before settling in 1834 in Rome. There the Order grew again in dignity and importance. Today it is a wholly Catholic organization with priories in Italy, Austria and Spain and associations in Great Britain and other countries. As it had from the outset so many centuries earlier, the Order maintains hospitals in these countries and involves itself in charitable works.

The eminence which the Sovereign Order of Malta enjoys today can be estimated from the fact that it is diplomatically represented in some fifty countries and that its Grand Master — who ranks in the Roman Church as a Cardinal — is in those countries given the honours due to a head of state. For the first time in more than four centuries, a knight from Britain — Fra Andrew Bertie — became Grand Master in 1988.

Other Knights of Malta

As has so often happened with the most honourable of institutions, unchivalrous individuals have found it possible and to their personal financial advantage to create, often on paper only, their own 'Sovereign Orders' of Malta and to persuade the gullible to pay quite large sums for 'diplomatic passports' and impressive titles. A newspaper article (*The Observer*, 15 March 1987) wrote of more than twenty such organizations, and of some of them in considerable detail.

It is a relief to be able to report that there exist also a number of quite unexceptionable bodies which draw their inspiration from the knights whom we have been discussing. There is, for instance, the Ancient and Illustrious Order, Knights of Malta, established in the United States in the 1880s on an authority from the Ancient and Loyal Illustrious Grand Black Order of Knights of Malta encamped at Glasgow. (We do not know whether the Scottish Order still exists.) That in America is not masonic, although many freemasons enjoy membership in what is an avowedly Protestant Christian organization. It has a large number of commanderies under its Supreme Commandery and it confers a range of twelve degrees.

Its charitable work includes the maintenance of a home for elderly members and their wives.

The Order of St. John in England

There is a special relationship between this Order of St. John and our United Orders. Its origin, development and purpose are given fuller treatment at Appendix F, where mention will also be made of the Sovereign Order of St. John of Jerusalem, a Roman Catholic organization which exists in this country.

[1] The precise span of the Middle Ages is difficult to pin down and reference books vary widely in their opinions. The years 1000 to 1400 seem to be generally agreed as the 'core' of the period, with an extension to about 1500.

3

THE EARLY MASONIC KNIGHTS TEMPLAR

When and where?

THE MASONIC HISTORIAN is well-accustomed to the scarcity of definitive early records. For instance, in the speculative Craft we have the oft-told story of Ashmole's initiation in 1646. His diary entry of the event lists 'those that were then of the lodge', but does this mean *on that occasion* or *already*? Had the lodge met before or was it a gathering of masons for a particular purpose? Norman Rogers tells us (*AQC* 65, 1952) about the men but can only conclude that 'they must have been initiated at some earlier date'.

Despite many earlier indications (including an unreliable Minute of 'The Lodge of Stirling Kilwinning' in 1743), the first unquestionable record of the admission of Royal Arch masons relates to a lodge at Fredericksburg, Virginia (which is still in existence), meeting on 22 December 1753, and here too we are left with the realization that those conferring the degree must already have been exalted. In 1769, in the Royal Arch Chapter of Friendship at Portsmouth (which itself dates from that year and survives as number 257), Thomas Dunckerley was able to make 'Mark Masons and Mark Masters', but where did he acquire the knowledge and authority to do so?

Similarly, while it can be safely assumed that the degree of Knight Templar had been practised in England and elsewhere for some time previously, the earliest existing Minute belongs to St. Andrew's Royal Arch Chapter at Boston, Massachusetts, and is also dated 1769. (That meeting is described at some length in chapter 16.)

In searching for the source or sources of the masonic Order of the Temple we are led inevitably to the continent of Europe. We are in great difficulty however in establishing places and dates. There are tantalizing glimpses: for instance it is said (*Gould's History of Freemasonry*, Poole's 1951 edition, volume 4, page 234) that two lodges in Germany were, in the 1740s, conferring chivalric *titles* upon their members – even on the Apprentices. Some writers prefer to base their studies on France. Ladislas de Malczovich (*AQC* 5, 1892, page 187) tells us, for example, that Chevalier Andrew Ramsay in his 'oration' of 1737 connected, without historical foundation, Freemasonry with the Crusades and with the chivalric Orders which arose therein. Malczovich continues: 'He [Ramsay] established three degrees, viz. (1) Ecossais; (2) Novice; (3) Knight Templar', but nothing is added to support that statement.

In the absence of irrefutable evidence one has to look firstly for possibilities and then to see whether the most promising of these can be regarded as a probability. By following such a procedure one arrives at the Rite of Strict Observance as a 'probable'.

The Rite of Strict Observance

This rite was predicated upon a legendary story of certain medieval Knights Templar who found asylum in Scotland when their Order was so brutally suppressed. These knights, it was said, became members of the masons' guilds and so were direct ancestors of the speculative fraternity now under the Grand Lodge of Scotland. By this route an unbroken succession of Templar Grand Masters, their names known only to a few, connected Jacques de Molay with the 1750s.[1]

Fuller accounts of the birth, life and death of the Strict Observance will be found in Gould's *History of Freemasonry* and elsewhere. For our present purposes it is sufficient to know that Karl Gotthelf, Baron von Hund (1722-76) was its creator and that woven into its fabric was an assumption that the time was ripe for the Templars to reveal to the world their continued existence, and even for them to lay claim to the former properties and privileges of the Order. Von Hund, who had become a freemason – probably in 1742, was according to his own later assertion received into the Order of the Temple (no evidence exists that this would have been a *masonic* Order) in Paris, in the presence of William, fourth and last Earl of Kilmarnock, who was Grand Master Mason of Scotland in 1742-3. Since Lord Kilmarnock, a Jacobite, was executed in 1746 for his support of Prince Charles Edward Stuart, that ceremony in Paris (*if* it took place) would have to have taken place in 1744 or thereabouts. We are to suppose that the Knights Templar present on that occasion, including of course the noble Earl, had been installed as such by the Scottish successors of the medieval refugees who have already been mentioned.[2]

We move on to the next decade (the 1750s) when the Strict Observance was being organized by von Hund and its first members were created. A feature of the obligation taken in its Entered Apprentice degree was an oath of unquestioning obedience to unknown superiors, hence the name of the rite – Strict Observance.

In 1763, the appearance in Germany of someone called Johnson – we do not know his forename – adds a bizarre note to the story. He declared himself to be an emissary of the Order of the Temple, authorized by the 'Sovereign Chapter' in Scotland to introduce the Order in Europe. The issue is complicated by the ready acceptance which many gave to Johnson's claim, but in due time von Hund overcame the intruder, who was eventually imprisoned without trial and died in 1775.

Von Hund was so successful with his rite that it almost superseded the English-style Freemasonry which had hitherto been active in Germany, and this despite the restrictive rules which had been added to that governance by 'unknown superiors'. But at the time there was a belief that the Templars were possessors of occult knowledge and many of the lodges and individuals who transferred their allegiance to von Hund's rite saw themselves as ultimately acquiring such knowledge. The Strict Observance was taken into other countries – Russia, France, the Netherlands, Switzerland and Italy – and until its demise in the 1790s it exerted considerable influence on the Continent, and strong elements from it can be found today in the Scandinavian and Rectified Scottish Rites (*see* chapter 17).

We have told its story – here greatly abbreviated – because of its bearing upon the development of the masonic Order of the Temple. Gould (in *Military Lodges 1732-1890*, 1899) took a quite positive view:

> Lodges in British regiments must have constantly worked side-by-side with the lodges under the Strict Observance . . . During the military operations, moreover . . . many prisoners were made on both sides, and that the masons among them fraternized in each case with their captors must be taken as a certainty.
>
> The degree of Knight Templar became a very favourite one in the lodges of the British army, and by these military and masonic bodies – who must have derived their knowledge of it from associating with the lodges and brethren under the Strict Observance – the degree was doubtless introduced into England and America.

George Draffen (*Pour la Foy*, 1949), in repeating Gould's words, points out that no evidence of an alternative source had come to light and, clearly, accepts Gould's theory as the best available.

The French Connection

The oft-mentioned 'Chapter of Clermont' (indeed Gould himself lends it some credibility) and the alleged Templar story of its sixth degree have been shown to be mythical (Jackson, *Rose Croix*, 1980) and have therefore no place in a list of possible sources. But a French origin cannot be entirely ruled out because there were lodges in London from 1736 onwards working in French and practising 'high degrees'. A Templar element therein, if there was one, would ante-date or be contemporary with von Hund's claimed admission to a Templar Order in about 1744, but — as already indicated — this was unlikely to have been masonic. It may have been more akin to Palaprat's Order, described in connection with the Charter of Larmenius at Appendix A.

The Rite of Seven Degrees

We have to consider also the Rite of Seven Degrees which emerged from the fertile brain of Lambert de Lintot (born in about 1736). Jackson (*Rose Croix*, 1980), in discounting its derivation from the 'Chapter of Clermont', supposes de Lintot to have adopted his system from a rite which in his day was operating in France, or to have created it by bringing together 'a mixture of degrees'. There is some uncertainty about when it came into being; Eric Ward (*AQC* 71, 1958, page 32) says 'from 1766 or earlier', although it is unlikely to have been so much earlier as to offer its seventh degree as a major source of our Order of the Temple. In any event, de Lintot's wordy 'Compendium' of his degrees (*AQC* 68, 1955, pages 99-101), drawn up in 1782, shows the seventh to have been a hotch-potch of Kadosh, Templar and many other elements.[3]

The Camp of Baldwyn at Bristol, partly because of Dunckerley's masonic involvements in the city (described in the next chapter), is sometimes proposed as a possible starting-point for our history but the first *authentic* reference to Knights Templar there appeared in the Minutes of the Sea Captains' Lodge No. 445 for 1783. That lodge, incidentally, a revival of an earlier lodge of the same name, survives by amalgamation within what is now known as the Royal Sussex Lodge of Hospitality No. 187, dating from 1796. (The Camp of Baldwyn is given fuller treatment at Appendix E.)

The Approach to 1791

Whatever may be concluded as to the origins of the degree of Knight Templar, it must be inferred that at the time (1769) when it was being worked in Massachusetts it was at that same period being practised elsewhere. In England, under the Grand Lodge of the Antients (formed in 1751), it was generally held that the Craft warrant conveyed powers to confer other degrees, such as those of Knight Templar and Rose Croix, in that sequence. The military lodges were in many cases also custodians of the chivalric degrees and it has to be remembered that the majority of these had been chartered by Ireland.

The earliest surviving record for England, however, is – like that for Massachusetts – within a Royal Arch context. The Chapter of Friendship at Portsmouth, in which (as already mentioned) Dunckerley had performed the Mark ceremonies nine years before, noted in its Minutes for 21 October 1778 that Dunckerley had advised them in writing that they 'might make Knight Templars' if they wanted to and so resolved. In the following year the 'Grand Lodge of All England' at York (1725-*c.*1792) is known to have conferred the degree, and may be suspected of having done so before.

We are now approaching the period when English knights were seeking means of assembly entirely separate from the Craft lodges or Royal Arch chapters within which they had themselves been created. Bristol – a much-used port of entry for travellers from southern Ireland – seems to have had one of the first such encampments, formed (according to Richard Smith, later to be 'Grand Superintendent' of Baldwyn, but now writing in about 1820) in 1784/5 as an offshoot of the Royal Arch Chapter of Charity. Other Baldwyn historians are convinced that that first Bristol encampment was established in, or prior to 1780 and that it was in fact the Baldwyn Encampment.

Since Thomas Dunckerley had been Grand Superintendent in and over Bristol since 1782 and, while still in that office, was to be instrumental in the events of 1791, we are in danger of infringing upon the next chapter of this book. But it must be added here that the Irish influence was probably seeping also through other ports, such as Liverpool, and that several of the old encampments remaining as preceptories on the roll of our present Great Priory date from this period. Others were established but did not survive; that of Observance of the Seven Degrees was a transformation of the remnants of de Lintot's rite; another with an interesting history was that of St. John of Jerusalem at Redruth. It was from among these that support was drawn for the Grand Conclave of 1791 whose bicentenary we are now celebrating.

Ireland

As will have become apparent, it is quite impossible to isolate the early history of the degree of Knight Templar in England from contemporary events in Ireland, and indeed in Scotland. As, at a later stage, the respective ruling authorities for the degree became associated more closely, we deem it worth while to survey, as briefly as we may, the Irish scene.

It may surprise the reader if we begin with as early a date as 1724, with the publication in Dublin of a pamphlet of a dozen or so pages entitled *A Letter from the Grand Mistress of the Female Free-Masons to Mr. Harding the Printer*. (John Harding did in fact print the original edition, although another followed in 1730, and the text was twice included in volumes of Jonathan Swift's collected works.) To Swift, that worthy Dean of St. Patrick's Cathedral, Dublin, is attributed the authorship of this parody, which was directed against James Anderson's first book of Constitutions, published in London in the previous year, 1723. On pages 8 and 9 of the booklet appears the paragraph here reproduced as printed:

> The Branch of the *Lodge* of *Soloman's* Temple, afterwards call'd the *Lodge* of St. *John* of *Jerusalem* on which our Guardian fortunately hit, is as I can easily prove, the Antientest and Purest now on earth. The famous old *Scottish Lodge* of *Killwinin* of which all the Kings of *Scotland* have been from Time to Time Grand Masters without Interruption, down from the Days of *Fergus*, who Reign'd there more than 2000 Years ago, long before the Knights of *St. John of Jerusalem* or the Knights of *Maltha*, to which two *Lodges* I must nevertheless allow the Honour of having adorn'd the Antient *Jewish* and *Pagan Masonry* with many Religious and Christian Rules.

Today, of course, Knights of St. John of Jerusalem and Knights of Malta are in our masonic context one and the same but we must credit the writer of these words with the intention to distinguish between two separate Orders. The passage here quoted is of interest because it attempts to link Freemasonry to the crusading Orders with which we claim at least a philosophical connection.

Lepper and Crossle's *History of the Grand Lodge of Ireland*, volume 1 (1925), provides some interesting dates for the first Irish references to masonic Knights Templar. Laurence Dermott, the volatile and verbose Grand Secretary and Deputy Grand Master of the Antients' Grand Lodge of England, said in his first Belfast edition of *Ahiman Rezon* (1782)[4] that it was at Fethard, County Tipperary, that Knight Templar masons were first made; Lepper and Crossle estimate that this 'must have been before 1764 (at least)'.

That statement is, of course, unsupported by evidence but the same authors reproduce the title-page of *The Rules of the High Knight Templars of Ireland*, approved in 1788, together with two pages of its text which list the names of ninety-three [surviving?] members, beginning with that of Edward Gilmore against a date of 24 March 1765, presumably that of his admission to the degree. The list seems consistent with a more general assertion by the authors that

> while the Grand Lodge of Ireland refused to recognize any degrees but those of the Craft, some of the best masons in Ireland were at the time propagating the higher degrees and endeavouring to persuade the Grand Lodge to take them under its protection. The degrees of Royal Arch, High Knight Templar and Prince Mason, i.e. Rose Croix, which last was introduced in the year 1782, were all being worked by bands of good and zealous masons, and there was hardly a Craft lodge in Ireland which did not come to have a knowledge of the two first-mentioned and appoint special nights for working them.

Those last words are borne out by a calendar for 1819 of Birr Lodge No. 163 IC which shows that, of the thirty-one meetings prescribed for the year, fourteen were for 'Blue Masonry' (the Craft), twelve for the Royal Arch and five for Knights Templar.

There survive certificates in great variety testifying to advancement in those days to degrees beyond the Craft. In several there is evidence of the sequence of events; for instance, in Lodge No. 568 (1779-1830), then at Boyle,

> . . . Randle Peyton has gone through the several degrees of Entered Apprentice, Fellow Craft, Master and Past Master and, having behaved judiciously and performed all his works with diligence and integrity amongst us, a Royal Arch Chapter was held in a full body to initiate him in the sublime degree of Excellent, Super Excellent, and, after a severe examination in the Royal Arch, his great zeal . . . having merited him the highest rank in Masonry, a General Conclave was to that effect assembled and, having sustained the amazing trials with fortitude and true valour, he was unanimously raised to the most sublime degree of High Knight Templar.

The seal of 'our Grand Lodge of High Knights Templars [*sic*] held in Boyle' is affixed as well as two of the Craft lodge, and the certificate is dated 1789.

This progression — 'passing the chair', a prerequisite to the Royal Arch, and the Royal Arch a necessary preliminary to the Templar degree — may be taken as typical of the period, not only in Ireland but wherever Knights Templar were being made.

It is interesting also to see floor-cloths of those days, some double-sided, which served both for the first three degrees and for those to which the aspiring Master Mason could hope to progress. The conferring of these additional degrees in Craft lodges persisted long after the establishment of authorities to warrant and control encampments of Knights Templar. At some stage the Grand Lodge issued an interdict against the working of anything beyond the third; in 1856 the charter of Lodge No. 652 at Lambeg was rescinded and the brethren of this and other lodges were suspended for having 'opened the chest' of the lodge 'and initiated one or more candidates to the high degrees of Masonry without a Warrant authorizing them to do so'.

In 1779 there was a Scottish invasion of Ireland, in masonic terms. Some Dublin brethren sought and obtained a warrant from the Lodge of Kilwinning (to which Swift made reference in 1724; it is now known as Mother Kilwinning No. 0 SC) for 'The High Knight Templars of Ireland Kilwinning Lodge'. We cannot here go into the curious history of Kilwinning, which includes periods of independence from Edinburgh. It must be said, however, that there was a popular belief that Kilwinning had the power to work and disseminate all possible varieties of 'high' degrees. This belief, like so many in Freemasonry, was of course based upon a misapprehension. That daughter-lodge in Dublin certainly misapprehended! For about two years it worked the usual sequence of degrees up to that of the Temple, but then made its peace with the Grand Lodge of Ireland and worked under one of its warrants until 1813.

It is all too often the case that the earliest records of Grand Lodges and their equivalents are missing or incomplete, and this is certainly true of the Early Grand Encampment of Ireland. In 1805 it *claimed* to have existed for more than a century, which would have meant that it ante-dated the premier Grand Lodge of England (1717) and that of Ireland (1725). Nevertheless there is sufficient reason to believe that it was the first genuine and comprehensive masonic Templar authority created in Ireland and, as its earliest traceable warrant was issued in 1793, it may be supposed that it was then fairly recently established. It has to be assumed also that it came into being through the efforts of knights who had received the degree in their lodges or Royal Arch chapters. It most certainly became very active and issued many warrants, including those soon to be mentioned for Scotland. Despite the existence by then of a Grand Conclave for England, the fifty-first Irish warrant was granted for an encampment at Scarborough in Yorkshire in 1809. This has not survived!

Scotland

It is tempting to wonder whether a trace of any medieval knighthood in Scotland was transmitted to the early speculative masons. There is a story, beloved of certain romantic historians of the Templars, that Prince Charles Edward Stuart was installed as Grand Master at Holyrood House, Edinburgh in 1745. It has to be admitted however that the first positive evidence of a 'Scottish' Templar degree being worked is that of 1769 in a lodge at Boston, Massachusetts; this has already been mentioned and the occasion will be described more fully in chapter 12. Thereafter, in Scotland itself, further ceremonies are documented, again under Craft warrants. For instance, the Lodge of Scoon and Perth (now No. 3 SC) travelled from Perth to Edinburgh in 1778 and there conferred the degree on the Master and office-bearers of St. Stephen's Lodge (now No. 145), which had been constituted in the previous year. This masonic knighthood seems to have been regarded as a highly-prized honour and there are interesting references to certain lodges in which *Craft* office could be held *only* by Knights Templar. One such lodge was that now known as Ayr St. Paul No. 204 SC, formed in 1799 for a regiment of Militia and no doubt travelling with it until it disbanded.

In the immediately preceding notes about Ireland we touched upon the Lodge of Kilwinning and its supposed entitlement to confer a variety of degrees. Undoubtedly, the mother-lodge and its daughters in Scotland exercised the 'privilege' and, since lodges under the Grand Lodge at Edinburgh were doing likewise, who shall say them nay!

Whether or not — and again it can only be deemed probable — Templar ceremonies in Scotland were derived from the regimental lodges of whatever constitution which were for the time being located there, we are well-informed as to the earliest chartered Knight Templar encampments north of the border. These obtained their authorities from Ireland and their so doing is attributed by

Draffen to the fact that so many of the travelling warrants within Scottish and English regiments had been issued by the Irish Grand Lodge. (It is relevant to add that the English Grand Conclave of 1791 was for many years a doubtful source of charters, whether for England, Scotland or elsewhere.)

It is believed that the first of these encampments was that at Aberdeen, established in 1794 by the Early Grand Encampment of Ireland,[5] and a further seventeen warrants for Scottish Knights Templar came from the same source up to 1822. The subsequent history will be summarized in a later chapter. But, many years later in 1904, a letter from the Recorder of the Early Grand Encampment of *Scotland* (formed in 1826) to a rival organization makes an unequivocal claim:

> Ours sprang from the working of the higher degrees by inner circles of the ordinary lodges. Our charters were, in the beginning of the nineteenth century (before yours, of course, had any existence), derived from an Irish source.

[1] There is an oral tradition that in 1314, when Robert Bruce reinstated the Royal Order of Scotland, he admitted all known Knights Templar to it (Gould/Poole, vol.4, page 216).

[2] It is sometimes said that the Rite of Perfection established at Clermont in 1754, from which developed the Emperors of the East and West in 1758, and thence in due course the Ancient and Accepted [Scottish] Rite, was but a Templar continuation of the French *écossais* (Scots) degrees. While the Kadosh degree, now the 30th of our present day rite, was in its original form concerned with the vengeance of the Templars for their persecution (a rather milder interpretation now prevails), none of the other degrees seems to have a link with the Order. The 27th, Commander of the Temple, has no legend and teaches no lesson (Jackson, *The Intermediate Degrees, 19°-29°*, 1982), although its tracing-board includes a suggestive cross.

[3] It is interesting to find that a plate of 1785 made by de Lintot (who was by trade an engraver) for his rite was adopted, with certain adjustments, by Dunckerley for use on Knight Templar certificates when the Grand Conclave was established in 1791 and remained in use for many years. It appears to this day on the summonses of the Royal Kent Preceptory No.20, which was constituted in 1812 at Newcastle-upon-Tyne. (*See* plates 2 to 4.)

[4] The date is given as 1783 in the text of the *History* but the title-page of *Ahiman Rezon* shows it to have been 1782.

[5] Draffen (*Pour la Foy*, 1949, p.203) disagrees with Sir Charles Cameron (*AQC* 13) as to the Aberdeen Encampment's origin, claiming it to have arisen within the Lodge of St George, now No. 190, at the time (1794) of its constitution. The present roll of Scotland's preceptories, however, gives 1794 as the date for St George Aboyne No 1, which resulted from an amalgamation in 1818 with Aboyne of 1812.

4

THE GRAND CONCLAVE, 1791-1805

IN 1791 THERE came into being the Grand Conclave of the Royal, Exalted, Religious and Military Order of H.R.D.M. Grand Elected Masonic Knights Templars [*sic*], K.D.S.H. of St. John of Jerusalem, Palestine, Rhodes, etc. To the studious freemason of today this rather comprehensive title has many implications. It would seem to embrace elements of the 18th and 30th degrees of our Ancient and Accepted Scottish Rite; Heredom also points in the direction of the Royal Order of Scotland, and the Order of Malta is clearly suggested. For the moment let us merely note these allusions and consider only how this sovereign authority, which we acknowledge to be the direct ancestor of our present Great Priory of the United Orders, was created.

Thomas Dunckerley: to 1790

In doing that we must immediately reintroduce the name of Thomas Dunckerley. Two excellent biographies exist of this outstanding character in masonic history, by Henry Sadler (1891) and Ron Chudley (1982). We are primarily concerned with his part in the establishment of the Grand Conclave but his involvement was possible only because, during the previous thirty years, he had pursued a career in Freemasonry which became progressively more distinguished. We must therefore tell you something of his earlier life.

He was born in modest circumstances in 1724 and it was not until many years had passed that he learned that he was a 'natural son' of King George II. Meanwhile he had entered the Royal Navy and had risen to the commissioned or warranted rank of gunner and schoolmaster. In 1767 the circumstances of his birth were made known to King George III, who granted him a pension from his own privy purse, and 'grace and favour' accommodation was allotted to him, firstly at Somerset House in the Strand, London, where he had been born, and later at Hampton Court Palace.

Dunckerley had been initiated in 1754 and, according to a letter of his many years later, had been made a Royal Arch Mason in the same year. While still in his thirties, he had clearly come to the notice of high masonic authority for by 1760 he was in possession of some kind of patent to 'inspect into the state of the Craft wherever he might go'. His seagoing duties took him to Canada where in 1760 he installed the first Provincial Grand Master at Quebec where, having obtained warrants from London, he established at least one lodge in a man-of-war. Another was similarly formed in 1762 in a ship at Portsmouth. These play no direct part in our story but it is worth noting that two of the warrants were used by Dunckerley after his retirement from the Navy to found stationary lodges in London which still exist.

Much more relevant is his appointment in 1767 as the first Provincial Grand Master for Hampshire because it was at Portsmouth that, two years later, is found early evidence of his interest in degrees beyond the Craft. We have already mentioned Dunckerley's visit in 1769 to the Royal Arch Chapter of Friendship in the town when he, having 'lately received the Mark', conferred that degree upon the companions. Of greater importance still is his letter of 1778 to the same chapter, authorizing them to 'make Knight Templars' if they wanted to do so. (By this time he had been appointed also the Royal Arch ruler of Hampshire whereas in 1769 he had been merely a visitor to the chapter.)

From 1777 onwards Dunckerley's masonic responsibilities grew until, by 1793, he was concurrently the Provincial Grand Master for eight Provinces and the Royal Arch Grand Superintendent in no fewer than eighteen, and it must be clearly understood that these appointments were by no means treated by him as sinecures. Let us turn to his Craft Province of Bristol which, when he received his patent in 1784, was combined with Gloucestershire and Somerset. It is perhaps indicative of his assiduity and popularity that in 1786, when the one Province was divided into three, he continued to rule all of them.

Dunckerley and the Knights Templar and of St. John

In Bristol (the only English city to have its own masonic Province) Dunckerley had ruled the Royal Arch from 1782[1] and, by 1791, his influence was well-established. There was at Bristol what is now called the Camp of Baldwyn, operating a Rite of Seven Degrees (*see also* Appendix E). R. M. Handfield-Jones in his booklet on the origin and history of our Orders (1973) writes that, in 1791

> . . . the Bristol knights *and many others from surrounding districts* approached Dunckerley with the suggestion that he should take the lead in forming *a Grand Encampment of Knights Templar for England and Wales.*

Eric Ward, however (in 'The Baldwyn Rite — An Impartial Survey', *AQC* 71, 1958, page 36) tells us that,

> in January 1791, Thomas Dunckerley, being Grand Superintendent of Royal Arch Masons at Bristol, was invited by the Knights Templar *in that city* to be *their* Grand Master, which he accepted.

These two statements conflict (we have used the italics to make this clear) and it would be as well to pause for a moment to consider the Bristol encampment, for at this time it was the *only* body conferring higher degrees in the city of Bristol.

While we cannot in this chapter enter into the controversy as to how and when it began, and as to how it adopted a rite of seven degrees, it was certainly in existence before 1791 and until that year had had as 'Grand Master' Joshua Springer, the Provincial Senior Grand Warden of Dunckerley's Provincial Grand Lodge of 1784. We can take it, therefore, that Dunckerley's *first* call to a Templar 'Grand Mastership' was to that of one encampment only, and that he was succeeding another in the office. And, in this Order and at this point in time, the term 'Grand Master' had no wider implication. The Camp of Baldwyn today lists Dunckerley as having succeeded to *its* Grand Mastership in 1791. All this suggests that Eric Ward was quite correct in his concise statement and that Handfield-Jones was perhaps a little too free in his rather broader assertion.

Before we move forward from the beginning of this, for us, very important year, let us look at New Year's Day, for Eric Ward — after writing the paper in *AQC* 71 from which we have quoted — discovered what he called 'striking evidence' that *on 1 January 1791* Dunckerley issued a patent. This was to a group of brethren in Bristol to whom, only eleven days before, he had (wearing the appropriate hat) granted a dispensation to form a Royal Arch chapter. The patent was for them to open 'a Conclave or Chapter of

Encampment at the City of Bristol of the Seven degrees of time immemorial'. The name adopted was the 'Eminent Chapter of Antiquity'. It is clear beyond a peradventure (since Eric Ward was not given to making such statements without solid foundation) that Dunckerley must have issued this patent on the very day on which he assumed power, and that it was purely a local creation. Ward tells us that the founders of both the Royal Arch chapter and the new encampment were in fact members of Baldwyn. The new body did not flourish and its knights afterwards returned to or joined Baldwyn. But it is interesting to find that Dunckerley's patent — which must have been the first issued for what was recognizably a Knight Templar encampment (with powers to confer other degrees) — was on the same lines as that sent to the Naval Encampment at Portsmouth (now Royal Naval Preceptory No. 2), constituted on 11 March 1791.

Dunckerley's correspondence in the first half of the year is revealing. A petition from the Conclave of Redemption at York (we have no date, but he replied to it on 22 March 1791) could well be interpreted as recognizing him as the head of an Order rather than merely asking him to become its own ruler. Let us look at his reply:

> I accept with gratitude the confidence you place in me as Grand Master by the Will of God, of the Most Noble and Exalted Religious and Military Order of Masonic Knights Templar of St. John of Jerusalem. I must request that as soon as possible you send to me the Names, Ages, Profession & Residence of all the Knights of your Encampment, as I intend to have a regular Register of our Order. Being Grand Superintendent of Royal Arch Masons at Bristol, I was requested by the Knights Templar in that City (who have had an Encampment time immemorial) to accept the office of Grand Master, which I had no sooner complied with than Petitions were sent to me for the same purpose from London 1, Bath 2, the first Regiment of Dragoon Guards 3, Colchester 4, York 5, Dorchester 6, and Biddeford [*sic*] 7. I suppose that there are many more Encampments in England, which with God's permission I may have the happiness to revive & assist. It has already been attended with a blessing for I have been but two months Grand Master & have already 8 Encampments under my care.[2]

Such a letter, and there are others in the same confident vein, leaves us in no doubt that — however the movement started — within a short space of time there was a Grand Master of a group of encampments and that there would soon be a Grand Conclave of Knights Templar.

Other correspondence with York at this time reveals Dunckerley's detailed interest in such matters as clothing and fees, no doubt engendered by the absence of anything like a Great Vice-Chancellor to act as his secretary! He introduced a 'signature of our Order' which was used for a while but did not meet with lasting success. It was a device, based upon that of the Royal Arch, which we now usually refer to as the Triple Tau but was in his day a capital 'T' resting upon the bar of a capital 'H', and standing for '*Templum Hierosolyma*'. By adding a capital 'E' to the design, thus:

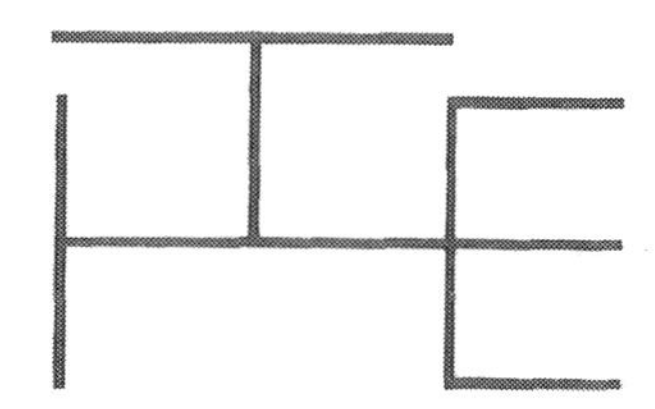

he amended its meaning to '*Templum Hierosolyma Eques*', not quite accurately translatable as 'Knight of the Temple at Jerusalem'.

Although in a letter of 21 April 1791 Dunckerley said that he expected to be succeeded as Grand Master in 1792 by the Duke of Clarence, who nearly forty years later became King William IV, that ambition was not to be realized. But he lost little time in seeking the encouragement of a more junior royal half-cousin, Prince Edward (later the Duke of Kent and Strathearn and the father of Queen Victoria). By the time that the first Grand Conclave was held, the Statutes then approved and printed (their text is reproduced at Appendix B) were able to record that 'Thomas Dunckerley, of Hampton Court Palace, in the county of Middlesex' was 'Grand Master of the Confraternity under the patronage of his Royal Highness PRINCE EDWARD'. Letters from the Prince, then stationed in Canada, written between 1792 and 1795 to Dunckerley, display a benign and genuine interest in the Order, which he himself ruled as Grand Master from 1805 to 1807, as we shall shortly discover, thereafter reverting to the office of Royal Grand Patron until his untimely death in 1820.

Grand Conclave Meets

On 24 June 1791, being the Feast of St. John the Baptist, the first Grand Conclave of the Order was held in London, and the installation of Thomas Dunckerley as Grand Master is recorded in our present-day *Liber Ordinis Templi* as having there taken place. His own report on the occasion is included in a letter written four days later to the Conclave at York:

> . . . on the 24th inst I went to Town and at 11 in the forenoon I met the Knights at St. Clements Church. At noon I opened a Grand Conclave at the Unicorn Tavern, with Lieut. General Sir Charles Rainsford, &c. We then made our Offerings for the poor, which was sent to the prisoners at the Savoy. Five Knights were install'd. I had compiled a Code of Laws from our Antient Statutes; which were unanimously approved. At 3, we ate the Bread of Thankfulness and drank the Cup of Cheerfulness. I appointed the Grand Officers; gave an exhortation and at 7 we departed in Love and Unity, Peace and Harmony.
>
> According to antient usage, I am very soon to be proclaimed on a high hill within a triangle of Knights Companions.

It is disappointing to be unable to discover if, when and where that interesting piece of ritual took place!

In the *Statutes* of 1809 were included lists of encampments both existing and defunct (*see* Appendix H) and among the latter were recorded three of those which had come under Dunckerley's wing in 1791. But the active roll shows that the first thirteen or fourteen then surviving were either 'time immemorial' (including Baldwyn at Bristol) or had been constituted by our first Grand Master and, of those, eight are still in being, not always under the original name.

The First Grand Master (1791-5)

We complained at the beginning of chapter 3 about the absence of definitive records and the lament continues with no less force now that our story has progressed to the early years of Grand Conclave. Here the frustration lies in that such records did exist but that in 1820 many, if not most, were consumed in a disastrous fire at the home of the then Grand Vice-Chancellor. What we know of Dunckerley's term of office as Grand Master (and indeed of succeeding periods) has had to be pieced together from secondary sources, and resort has had to be made here and there to presumption.

We would like to know more of the way in which some of the first encampments of the Order were established, and of when, why and how those which did not long survive had to be removed from the register. Dunckerley quite obviously laboured long at his desk and we would want to see more of his letters. One can only be thankful that the Ancient Conclave of Redemption were able to preserve much of their correspondence with the Grand Master (and good use has been made of it in writing this book). It must be said again that Dunckerley appears effectively to have been his own 'Vice-Chancellor' and he must have written an enormous number of courteous letters to the encampments, and to individual members, in discharging most conscientiously what he conceived to be his duty to the Order. And this, remember, when he was also communicating with no less devotion with his Provinces in the Craft and Royal Arch.

But he was not content to administer *in absentia*; there is evidence – and much more may well exist in those Provinces – of his travelling around the country on masonic affairs. Those of us who make good use of the Inter-City service of British Rail, and even of air travel, should spare a thought for our first Grand Master in the uncomfortable coaches, on roads which were often rough and dangerous, which would have been his only means of paying those visits.

In honouring, as we do, those of the early encampments which have survived to this day, we should perhaps regard them as a monument to the faithful service of Sir Knight Thomas Dunckerley.

A Brief Interregnum

William Hannam assumed charge, on Dunckerley's death, of the Order's affairs. He was a man of some consequence, being the Provost Marshal of His Majesty's Guards, and he had served as Grand Master, in 1790, of the Rite of Seven Degrees which was mentioned in chapter 3. Now, signing himself 'Acting Gd. Master', he advised the encampments of the loss which they had sustained and put forward a suggestion as to his successor.

> Permit me to Point out as the Person Most Eligible to do Honour to the Society The Rt Hon'ble Lord Rancliffe, who is a Member of the Chapter and Conclave of Observance. The more so from being a Colonel in the Army.

A sufficiency of the Knights Companions presumably indicated their approval and the noble Lord was elected and installed on 3 February 1796.

The Second Grand Master (1796-1800)

Thomas, the first Lord Rancliffe, cuts a rather insignificant figure in the story of our United Orders and for this we must to some extent blame the scanty records of his Grand Mastership. We know that he was born Thomas Boothby Parkyns in 1755 into a wealthy family. He followed a parliamentary career, sitting firstly for Stockbridge in Hampshire and then as the Member for Leicester. When fears arose of a Napoleonic invasion of England, Rancliffe raised the Prince of Wales's Regiment of Fencibles and it was in command thereof that he gained his colonel's rank. (The regiment, incidentally, had a short-lived Antient lodge in 1798, but its seems improbable that Rancliffe, who was a 'Modern', had anything to do with it.) His peerage was Irish and so he was able to sit in the House of Commons until his death.

As a freemason he comes to notice as the first Provincial Grand Master for Nottinghamshire in 1783, to which responsibility was added the Provinces of Derbyshire, Leicestershire and Rutland in 1789. In the Royal Arch he became the Grand Superintendent in and over Leicestershire and Rutland in 1793, although he had been elected Second Grand Principal in the previous year. He continued to rule the Province when he became Grand Z in 1794, holding both offices until his death in 1800. All this would seem to indicate great zeal for the fraternity but J. T. Thorp, writing in more recent times in *The Transactions of the Leicester Lodge of Research*, said that

> . . . he does not appear to have taken the slightest personal interest in Masonry in this Province during the eleven years that he presided over it, except on one solitary occasion, namely being present at an Emergency Meeting of St. John's Lodge, Leicester, on April 27th 1791, after which he presented the set of silver jewels for the officers, which are still in use.

It is possible that he devoted more time and energy to his governance of the Royal Arch.

With the rule of the Order of the Temple, he also succeeded to Dunckerley's Grand Commandership in the Society of Antient Masons of the Diluvian Order or Royal Ark and Mark Mariners, but it is improbable that he gave much attention to it.

It is recorded that the Templar Grand Conclave met twice in his first year and but once in each of the three following. One suspects an absence of enthusiasm in this Grand Master for the Order of the Temple; an encampment at Ashton-under-Lyne was warranted by him on 12 August 1796 but it was to be almost nine years before another came into being. Perhaps his parliamentary duties and the management of his estate occupied so much of his time that he could spare little for what was then a relatively new masonic fraternity. And in 1799, of course, the Unlawful Societies Act led to a temporary panic among freemasons, until the 4th Duke of Atholl (for the Antients) and the Earl of Moira (of the premier Grand Lodge) persuaded the Government to insert a saving clause.

Robert Gill

On the death of Lord Rancliffe it was Robert Gill, then Deputy Grand Master, who for more than four years acted in his place. The Grand Conclave was, however, in abeyance and the Act of 1799 just mentioned may have been to some extent responsible for that. Gill had served as Senior Grand Warden in the Antient Grand Lodge in 1796 and was again in that office (1798-1801). It is interesting to realize that although, at this period, the two persuasions in the Craft and Royal Arch still had their differences it was possible in the Order of the Temple for members from both to work in harmony at all levels.

The Duke of Kent, still Royal Grand Patron, was abroad on duty until 1803 and it was not until the following year, possibly with the Duke's approval, that Gill enlivened the situation with a circular letter to the encampments:

London, 23rd October 1804

Brethren and Sir Knights
It is with infinite concern and regret that I now inform you that the Grand Conclave has been dormant for at least six years, to the great detriment of the Order and to the Brethren Sir Knights Companions in general.

I am therefore directed by the members of the Encampment No. 20 of the 'Holy Cross of Christ', under our Grand Commander the Duke of Kent (being the only Encampment in London, meeting at the Queen's Arms Tavern, Newgate Street) to state that it is their intention to form and congregate themselves into a Grand Conclave, for a revival thereof: presuming it will meet your concurrence and approbation, as we hope of the other Encampments in the country.

Permit me therefore, Brother Sir Knights, to request the favour of an immediate reply on or before the second Monday in next month, being the night of our Encampment, with your Sentiments and Support thereto.

The outcome of this move is amply reported in another letter, written less than four months afterwards:

> At a General Meeting, holden on the 14th of January 1805, a Deputation was appointed to wait upon H.R.H. the Duke of Kent, for the purpose of obtaining his approbation and consent to the drawing up of a Charter of Compact between the Members of this Order and H.R.H. as their Head or Chief. The Deputation had the honor to meet H.R.H. agreeable to his own appointment, on Sunday the 20th of January at Kensington Palace when the proposal not only met H.R.H's full approbation and consent, but he condescended to be nominated Most Eminent and Supreme Grand Master of the Order.
>
> Whereupon another General Meeting was called, and a Committee was appointed to compose and draw up the Charter of Compact above alluded to, which has been done in as full and ample a manner as possible and which has met with the entire approbation of H.R.H. and wherein he has condescended to be nominated M.E. & S.G.M. of the Order, and the Knights Companions in it are to be the first Grand Officers for the year ensuing, viz:
>
> | | |
> |---|---|
> | ROBERT GILL Esq | Deputy and Acting Grand Master |
> | JAMES HIGGINS M.D. | First Grand Captain |
> | EVAN LLOYD | Second Grand Captain |
> | WILLIAM DAVIS | Grand Chancellor |
> | JOHN GILBERT | Grand Scribe and Register |
> | JAMES MURRY | |
> | JOHN SAFFELL | Grand Standard Bearers |
>
> Having thus informed you of the very forward and we trust very pleasing and prosperous state of the Order, I would beg leave to advert to some of the Powers and Prerogatives conferred by H.R.H. on the Grand Conclave; the first and most important of which is, that they now have full right and authority to grant Warrants for new Encampments, and to exact from all others a strict account for registering fees; to grant Certificates &c. — Secondly That there is to be an Annual Grand Conclave of Communication to which the Principals of all Encampments are to be invited for the Election of Grand Officers, and for all other general purposes of the Order. Besides there is to be a Quarterly Communication for the purposes of Charity, and to regulate the public business of the Order.
>
> Being thus in possession of our proceedings and of the Powers wherewith we are invested let us beg that you will be so kind as to favour us with your correspondence, and we will thank you to remit any registering fees, that may be now due, from your Encampment to the Grand Conclave, addressed to the G.S. and Reg., as under, and we will thank you to send us a list of all the Encampments that you now know of lest we should have omitted sending to all, when you acknowledge receipt of this, which we trust will be immediately after your next Meeting.

One more thing I have to inform you of; that it is the request of H.R.H. and is inserted in the body of the Charter that the Jewels and Regalia are to be worn as follows, viz: the Grand Commander a Star of eight points with a black Sash over the right shoulder; the Captains a similar Sash with a Star of seven points; Private Companions the same Sash with a Mother of Pearl Cross, and all to wear an Apron bound with black with the proper badge or Skull and Cross-bones displayed thereon; and for the sake of uniformity we think that a Suit of Black and black Sword would be more consistent with the Order than any other dress.

By Command of the D.G.M. and Grand Officers,
I am, with all due respect,
Your Brother and Companion,
JOHN GILBERT G.S. & Reg.

Blackwall
February 14, 1805

Although the Charter of Compact to which this letter refers has survived in the archives, it is framed behind glass and is somewhat difficult to read. It is also a rather lengthy document. For these reasons, and because it was before long to be revoked, it has been thought preferable to reproduce only John Gilbert's letter for this conveys all that is significant in the Charter. (The full text of the Charter was printed in C. F. Matier's *The Origin and Progress of the Preceptory of St. George 1795-1895* (1910), of which there are several copies in the archives.)

[1] Although biographies and reference-books (including Bristol's own Year Books and those of the United Grand Lodge until some twenty-five years ago) agree on 1782, the *Masonic Year Book Historical Supplement* (2nd ed., 1969, page 360) unaccountably gives 1793.

[2] Dunckerley was a little premature in claiming eight under command; the petition from Colchester was withdrawn.

5

THE GRAND CONCLAVE, 1805-1846

WE COME TO a period in the story of the United Orders into which two royal brothers, The Dukes of Kent and Sussex, enter very prominently, and the latter's Grand Mastership in particular deserves careful examination because of the charges which have been levelled against it. Other eminent knights, of course, played their parts and there are two in particular who deserve our respect and gratitude.

The Duke of Kent

We closed the previous chapter with a description of how the Royal Grand Patron, normally a remote figure in any masonic hierarchy, agreed to assume the Grand Master's throne and, in doing so, ended a period of stagnation and uncertainty. Prince Edward Augustus, who had in 1799 been created Duke of Kent and Strathearn, was in many respects the right man for the job. Born in 1767, he had been initiated in the Union Lodge at Geneva at the age of 23. As is traditionally the practice, he was in the same year, 1790, made a Past Grand Master of the premier Grand Lodge, often described as 'the Moderns', and was also appointed Provincial Grand Master for Gibraltar and Andalusia. He was on the active list of the army and was, it cannot be gainsaid, a martinet whose strictness sometimes got him into trouble with the military authorities at home. It was this characteristic which caused him to be relieved of his command on the Rock and he was posted to North America where he became the Provincial Grand Master for Lower Canada under the *Antient* Grand Lodge and it was from there that his correspondence, as Patron, with Dunckerley was dated between 1792 and 1795.

His return to England in 1803 enabled Gill, as we have seen, to enlist his aid in reviving the Grand Conclave but, before considering his role in our Orders, let us remind ourselves of the Duke of Kent's other place in masonic history. Having, as we have seen, a foot in both camps it is not surprising that he was one of many who wished to bring the rival Grand Lodges of the Craft into harmony. His acceptance of the Grand Mastership of the Antients in 1813, at which time his brother of Sussex was assuming equivalent office in the Moderns, smoothed the way to the Union which took place at the end of that year. Sussex became the first ruler of the United Grand Lodge while Kent, a Past Grand Master since 1790, retired gracefully to the renewed enjoyment of that distinction.

At the time when Robert Gill was able to report, in 1805, the Duke's accession to the Grand Mastership of the Order, it seems that none of those involved were in possession of a copy of the Statutes or Constitutions which Dunckerley had drawn up for approval at that first meeting of Grand Conclave on 24 June 1791 (*see* Appendix B). Those Constitutions later came to light and, in 1807 – with the full approval of the Duke – it was possible to elect as Grand Master Waller Rodwell Wright and for the Duke to revert to his more appropriate role of Royal Grand Patron. It took some little time for this to be finalized, and this was done in some style in 1809 by a 'Charter of Constitution', beautifully engrossed on parchment or vellum.

This document should be regarded as one of the treasures of our present Great Priory's archives and, because of its importance and its bearing upon the provenance of our United Orders of today, the full text of the Charter is reproduced at Appendix C. It decreed that the earlier 'Charter of Compact' , referred to in the previous chapter, was revoked and that the Order was once again regarded as founded upon the 1791 Statutes. This, of course, reinforces the point that we are in 1991 commemorating the bicentenary both of the first Grand Conclave and of the Constitutions which were then accepted as governing the Knights Templar who then and thereafter placed themselves under the authority of the Grand Conclave. During the short but significant rule of the Duke of Kent several new encampments were established, three of which are still working. Thus the stagnation of the 'lean years' was ended and we must therefore be grateful to the Duke for his role in bringing that about. It will have given him great satisfaction to have been able to witness, during the years immediately following, the further strengthening of the Order.

Through a late dynastic marriage to the widowed Princess Victoria of Leiningen the Duke earned a place in British royal history because in 1819 a child was born to them. Sadly, in the following year and at the age of only 53, the Duke died at Sidmouth in a charming house, then known as Woolbrook Cottage but now the very pleasant Royal Glen Hotel. His infant daughter was in 1837 to begin her long reign as Queen Victoria.

Waller Rodwell Wright

Here is one of many names to conjure with in the further history of the United Orders, and indeed in a much wider masonic context. When, on 12 April 1807, he was elected and installed as Grand Master, he was already the Acting Grand Commander and his succession to the throne could scarcely have been in doubt. Thanks to Desmond Caywood's researches (published in *AQC* 85) and to Colin Dyer's important discovery of Wright's ritual manuscripts, we now know a great deal more about him.

Born in 1775 at Bury St Edmunds in Suffolk, he was called to the Bar and thereafter served twice as Recorder of his native city (1801-3 and 1806-14), was Consul-General of the Ionian Islands (1803-6) and later became Senior Justice in Malta from 1814 until his death there in 1826.

In Freemasonry, he was initiated at Bury St Edmunds in a lodge no longer existing and thereafter joined the important Lodge of Antiquity (now No. 2) and the Prince of Wales's Lodge (No. 259) in London. In the Royal Arch he was appointed Grand Superintendent of Suffolk in 1801 and of Cambridgeshire in 1807, although he made way in the latter office for the Reverend George Adam Browne in 1810. The former he retained, for quite long periods *in absentia*, until his death. But he rose also to higher rank, as 'Grand Master J' (3rd Grand Principal) in the Grand Chapter of the Moderns in 1802-3 and again in 1806-12. A somewhat curious appointment in the Craft came his way in 1813 as Provincial Grand Master of the Ionian Islands; curious firstly because he was no longer residing there and secondly because it was not until 1861 that an English lodge was formed there (still working). Rather in advance of his arrival as a Judge, he was issued with a Patent as Provincial Grand Master of Malta (the Province had a number of different titles during his stewardship) and retained the office until his death.

While Grand Master of our Orders, he was also the founder and Grand Master of the Order of the Red Cross of Palestine, long since defunct, and on the eve of his departure to Malta he installed the Duke of Sussex as his successor in both. He left the Knights Templar in England in good heart and it is worthy of note that, among the masonic events in Malta during his fourteen-year term, was the founding of the Melita Encampment (Preceptory) in 1815. In recent years, that has been transferred to England and meets in Hertfordshire.

By the end of Waller Rodwell Wright's Grand Mastership there were forty-eight encampments on the roll of Grand Conclave and, of those constituted in his time, eight are still with us.

Grand Conclave Meetings

It would be as well to pause for a moment to make the point that the Grand Conclave, having been restored to an active role in 1805, met on many occasions until 1812. It appears that only the annual conventions, those at which the Grand Officers for the year were invested, summoned the knights generally; for the others only the Grand Officers, together with any members of the Order whose presence was especially required, were called upon to attend. Here at last we have some definitive records in the form of printed proceedings from 1807 onwards. After two meetings at St Paul's Coffee House by the Cathedral the next set of Minutes shows that a move had been made to Freemasons' Tavern, on the site of the Freemasons' Hall of today in Great Queen Street.

In those of 12 April 1810, we can sense a growing irritation with the lodges and chapters which were still dispensing the chivalric degrees.

> . . . Several Crafts [*sic*] Lodges, held at Wigan and Warrington . . . (having no lawful Warrant of this Order), were clandestinely installing Knights Templars; also a Crafts Lodge at Bury.

Stern measures were required: the Grand Master waited upon the Royal Grand Patron. H.R.H. was pleased to issue a Proclamation, 'copies of which were distributed to different parts of the country, to put a stop to such practices.' One wonders to what extent it succeeded!

Of perhaps greater interest is the account of the 'Grand Conclave of Emergency of Grand Officers' held on 30 January 1812, when the Duke of Kent arrived.

> upon which the Grand Officers arranged themselves in due order for his reception: His Highness [*sic*] was afterwards introduced by the two Grand Experts and two Aid du Camps [*sic*], and conducted to the Throne in solemn form.

But that was by no means the only notable feature of the programme. H.R.H. the Duke of Sussex was then similarly introduced 'and conducted to his situation at the right of the M.E. Grand Master'.

The Minutes of the previous meeting having been read and confirmed, yet another illustrious freemason was to appear and the record of this event is worth quoting in full:

> The Right Honourable Francis Earl MOIRA having been proposed, ballotted for, and approved on the 23rd instant, and this meeting being convoked for the purpose of installing his Lordship, the Noble Earl having therefore attended the Encampment, he was accordingly introduced by the Grand Orator, Provost and Hospitaller, and reported by the Senior Captain of the Lines: His Lordship was afterwards installed a Knight Templar, according to antient form. The Grand Orator was pleased to explain the rise, progress, and principles of the Order.

And then

> His Royal Highness the Grand Patron was pleased to appoint His Royal Highness Frederick Augustus DUKE of SUSSEX to be Captain General of the Order.

This Minute is noteworthy for two features: it has the Duke of Sussex's forenames in the wrong order and it tells us that, for this rather special occasion, the Royal Grand Patron usurped the prerogative of the Grand Master by making the appointment!

At the next Grand Conclave but one, on 5 May, the Grand Master, Waller Rodwell Wright, proposed that the Duke of Sussex should succeed him. The Deputy Grand Master, John Burckhardt, seconded and the motion was carried unanimously.

On 6 August 1812 the Duke was installed and, on entry into the assembly, was 'conducted under the Arch of Steel to a chair which had been prepared for him'. After describing, in quite considerable detail, the ensuing ceremony, the Minutes tell us that

> His Royal Highness, in an eloquent speech, returned his thanks to the Knights assembled, assuring them of his zealous attachment to the principles, and determination to maintain the privileges, and promote the well being, of the Order.

Doubts have been expressed as to whether the Duke wholly fulfilled those undertakings, but more of than anon.

We are fortunate indeed in that some, at least of the Proceedings of Grand Conclave in this period were printed because the originals would almost certainly have been lost by fire. It was clearly the practice for Grand Officers, and probably all encampments, to receive copies for among those in our archives is an uncut double folio comprising the Minutes of two successive meetings; it was folded and sent through the post to Hippolyte Joseph da Costa, the Junior Grand Captain.

There are other names of great interest to the masonic student to be found in these Minutes: William Henry White, joint Grand Secretary, with his father, of the premier Grand Lodge from 1809 to 1813, who thereafter served the United Grand Lodge until 1856; Edwards Harper, Deputy Grand Secretary of the Antients, who from 1813 to 1838 worked with White as joint Grand Secretary of the United Grand Lodge; the Reverend Samuel Hemming; Simon McGillivray. These and other names reinforce the important truth that, while the Antient and Modern persuasions prolonged their separatism until 1813, many of their leading protagonists managed nonetheless to enjoy perfect harmony within chivalric Masonry. And those last two words lead us naturally into the next stage of our story.

The Duke of Sussex

One is sorely tempted to expatiate upon the masonic activity of HRH Augustus Frederick, Duke of Sussex, because it makes fascinating reading. Fortunately, because of his great services from 1813 until his death in 1843 as the first Grand Master of the United Grand Lodge of England, full justice to his Craft and Royal Arch career has been done by many writers. Here we will confine ourselves to mentioning that this sixth son of King George III was born in 1773 and was initiated in 1798 in Lodge *zur siegenden Wahrheit* in Berlin, still meeting there as No. 185 under the United Grand Lodges of Germany.

The Duke's Problems

We must remind ourselves, however, that – having been appointed Deputy Grand Master of the premier Grand Lodge in 1812 – he accepted the Grand Mastership in the following year as the final move towards union of the two jurisdictions. For its consummation, the most senior representatives of the two parties to it signed the 'Articles of Union' which are to this day deemed to be carried in procession into and out of Grand Lodge by the Grand Registrar.[1] It is Article II to which we must pay particular attention. As every freemason is supposed to know, because the words appear at the head of the Constitutions, it prescribed that

> pure Ancient Masonry consists of three degrees and no more; Viz. those of the Entered Apprentice, the Fellow Craft and the Master Mason, including the Supreme Order of the Holy Royal Arch.

Less well-known is the fact that Article II went on to say:

> But this Article is not intended to prevent any Lodge or Chapter from holding a meeting in any of the degrees of the Orders of Chivalry, according to the constitutions of the said Orders.

This provision can be interpreted in various ways. Lodges and chapters under both the Antients and the Moderns (and under Ireland and Scotland) had long been holding such meetings and, perhaps on a more limited scale, would continue to do so for several decades more. Article II surely gave its blessing to such a practice, although in 1817 Grand Lodge and the then newly-formed Grand Chapter seem to have withdrawn themselves from that part of it.

Less apparent is an implied approval or recognition of the existence of sovereign masonic authorities for controlling chivalric degrees. Indeed it simply is not there.

Here, then, were uncertainties to be faced by the Duke of Sussex and the Knights Templar and it has been said – unfairly – that the Duke's solution was to neglect and thus give the impression that he disliked the Order. It was also claimed, wrongly, that he was a monotheist (on grounds which we need not here pursue) but he could scarcely have taken with honour his obligations as a member and as Grand Master if he did not hold to the Trinitarian Christian faith. As we have elsewhere mentioned, he was also an active member of the non-masonic Order of the Temple which Fabré-Palaprat had established on the basis of the Charter of Larmenius, and that too demanded an unwavering belief in the Holy Trinity.

We must in all fairness recognize the delicate position in which he was now placed. There was in the Craft a strong faction which resolutely opposed the idea that any kind of Freemasonry could exist beyond the three degrees and the Royal Arch. (Here and there successors to that faction survive amongst us!) The masonic and chivalric brethren were relatively few in number and yet, to survive against the Unlawful Societies Act of 1799, they had somehow to remain within a masonic context. The Duke was at the head of both of the seemingly irreconcilable elements and wished to offend neither, nor did he relish the idea of resigning from either or both of the high offices for he loved Freemasonry in all its forms.

R. M. Handfield-Jones in his excellent booklet of 1973, *The Origin and History of the United . . . Orders*, believes that the Duke's solution was 'quietly and unostentatiously' to 'take unofficial action to keep the Temple alive until a more settled and favourable time should arise'. This opinion is surely correct.

The Duke's Solution

It seems likely that his first thought was to remove Grand Conclave from sight, and this is borne out by the fact that reference to only one meeting of it, on 31 January 1820, is on record during a period of twenty years or more. He ensured nevertheless that business, as it arose, was carried on by his Deputy Grand Master, J. C. Burckhardt, and the Grand Vice-Chancellor and Registrar, Robert Gill. This business included, of course, keeping in touch with existing encampments and also the operation of an innocent device by which dispensations could be granted for the opening of new ones pending the issue, at some future date, of a proper warrant.

It is not easy nowadays to find evidence prior to 1824 that this device was actually employed, but G. E. W. Bridge's invaluable notes inform us that he had

> found traces of a number that were founded, worked and died during the period, leaving no trace except a Dispensation still on a lodge wall, old papers in a lodge box, or a reference in the records of another body.

If they were recorded on a roll by Robert Gill, that roll must also have gone up in flames in 1820 when his house in Soho Square was burnt down. A tragedy for Gill, who had served the Order so long and so well, and who did not long survive this disaster. An irreparable loss to our archives of today because so many tantalizing questions can never be answered.

We do know, however, of three new encampments which arose in 1824, 1826 and 1830 respectively and this must have offered some small encouragement to those who were keeping the standards unfurled.

It was during this period also, in 1819, that an extraordinary attempt was made to involve the Duke of Sussex in setting up a Supreme Council of the Ancient and Accepted Rite. The effort was an unworthy one and it was effectively suppressed.

By wisely fostering, so far as he could, an illusion that Knights Templar scarcely existed, and by keeping up that pretence until it could safely be abandoned, the Duke very probably ensured the future of our Order.

The Restoration

We do not know precisely when but, at some time in the early 1830s, the Grand Master decided that the risks which had been present in 1813 and the immediately following years could be ignored and he himself publicly assumed control. It was undoubtedly a worthy tribute to him that what appears to have been the first warrant to be granted, in this new lease of life, was for the Royal Sussex Encampment at Torquay in 1834. I have entered the caveat because Bridge's notes make reference to a 'Coteswold Encampment of the Seven Degrees' at Cheltenham which he thinks may have been warranted by the Duke in 1833. Not having seen his evidence for this, it seems to me more likely that, with the significant qualification in its title, it had more to do with Baldwyn at Bristol, which was at this time enjoying a period of independence from Grand Conclave.

A few other warrants followed before the long reign of the Grand Master ended with his death on 21 April 1843.

John Christian Burckhardt

We can now bring into some prominence the name of a worthy brother knight who, as Deputy Grand Master from 1807, had ably supported both Waller Rodwell Wright and the Duke of Sussex. He was now to serve as Acting Grand Master until 1846, which would bring his tally of years at the centre of our Order's affairs to the very creditable total of thirty-nine.

Burckhardt had been born at Leyden in the Netherlands in 1772 and, coming to England, had entered Freemasonry in his early twenties. He became a member of the Lodge of Antiquity, and was associated with William Preston and his Lectures, so his is yet another name familiar to masonic students.

Some time was to elapse before Grand Conclave would assemble to elect a successor to the Duke of Sussex. Burckhardt himself, now over 70 years old, certainly had no ambitions in that respect but, with so much experience behind him, he was able to keep everything on an even keel. Only about thirty encampments seem to have been in full touch with the centre at this stage and information was sought as to others which might have survived through the 'difficult' era. Some that were 'in abeyance' were stirred into renewed activity and brought in new members. Burckhardt himself, folowing the Duke's example of warranting without reference to Grand Conclave, chartered two encampments, signing 'in the absence of a M.E. & Supreme Grand Master, J. C. Burckhardt, Pt. Dep.Gd.Master and Grand Sub-Prior'. To that last rank he had been appointed *ad vitam* by the Duke of Sussex in 1812. When he was able to propose the name of the next Grand Master, he summoned Grand Conclave on 27 February 1846 and nominated Colonel Charles Kemeys Kemeys Tynte, who was duly elected and was, on 3 April installed.

Burckhardt, having performed that ceremony, gratefully retired from active office. He had nobly borne the heat of many days and, it is said, at no small financial loss to himself. At his death in 1848 his widow passed some of his papers to the Lodge of Antiquity, but no others have survived to cast more light upon our history.

[1] The document is now considered to be too precious to be folded and carried in the Grand Registrar's splendidly embroidered bag.

6

WHENCE AND WHITHER THE ROSE CROIX?

LET US CALL a halt, for a while, in the relentless march of the years and even retrace our steps, for we have just passed an important milestone – one at which a significant change in practice, if not in direction, can be perceived.

Additional Degrees

Even before Dunckerley succeeded in establishing the Grand Conclave in 1791, it was by no means unusual to find Craft lodges and Royal Arch chapters working 'additional' degrees.[1]

We will not attempt to list the degrees, for we are here concerned only with Christian Freemasonry; remember only that under various Grand Lodges – premier, York, Antient, Irish and Scottish, and even that of Wigan – a Templar/Malta ceremony was being performed within daughter-lodges. Royal Arch chapters, perhaps quite casually at first, took over this ceremony and this no doubt accounts for the qualification which to this day is required of candidates in our preceptories, but there is not too much logic in connecting the story of *Zerubbabel's* Temple, which is commemorated in a degree available to non-Christians, with that of the Hospitallers and Templars which is set so many centuries later.

Be that as it may, the next development was when the Rose Croix degree, imported from France, was added above that of the Temple and Malta and the even more elevated rituals of the *Templar* Kadosh and the Ne Plus Ultra[2]. We need not now concern ourselves with the extent to which these changes had taken place before Dunckerley came on the scene. The title which he gave to our Order (to which reference was made at the beginning of chapter 4) can readily be interpreted as embracing Rose Croix and Kadosh and we have later evidence in the form of certificates (an example is illustrated at plate 5) that the Ne Plus Ultra element was there.

In the Early Encampments

So until 1845 — and in some cases beyond that year — a member of an encampment had every reason to expect that, after admission as a Knight Templar and Knight of Malta, he would in time be advanced to a higher level.

It would be as well, since we have travelled back into these earlier days, to note that the encampments took many years to be regarded as the exclusive practitioners of the chivalric Orders. As has been the case since time began, die-hards clung to ancient privileges for as long as possible.

I am grateful to E. B. H. Chappell, of the Royal York Lodge of Perseverance No. 7, for an interesting (and, I suspect, not untypical) echo from 1810 of a masonic excursion. In the Minutes of the Lodge of Hope No. 4 of the Antients, from which the present No. 7 enjoys unbroken descent, is recorded a visit 'in form, by the Knights Templar from the encampment of the Cross of Christ' (now St. George's Preceptory No. 6). True, it was an Antient lodge and perhaps more likely to maintain official links with a body of freemasons both Antient and Modern, but the event also demonstrates the willingness of our knightly forefathers, whether or not they had the blessing of their Grand Conclave, to take their encampment on what might conceivably be regarded as a recruiting drive! Such practices and such intentions are today perfectly normal among our brethren in the United States.

Robert Crucefix

The mention of the Cross of Christ Encampment prompts me to introduce one of its later members, Doctor Robert Thomas Crucefix (he joined it in 1831 shortly after his installation in Edinburgh in the Scottish Grand Conclave). You must look elsewhere for his story in more detail (*The Freemasons' Pocket Reference Book* by Fred Pick and Norman Knight, 3rd ed., rev. Frederick Smyth, 1983, is a convenient source); suffice it to say here that he was involved in the foundation of what became the Royal Masonic Benevolent Institution, and that in this matter he fell foul of the Duke of Sussex.

He produced, primarily as a forum in which to publish his arguments (and argumentative he was!), *The Freemasons' Quarterly Review* (1834-49). In this he gave vent to his dissatisfaction, undoubtedly shared by others, at the apparent inaction in the chivalric Orders: 'Nothing is being done about the Grand Conclave because there are only three officers, of whom one, the Duke of Sussex, is dead'. Clearly he was one who misjudged the late, lamented Grand Master in this respect.

This irritation was, undoubtedly, one of the factors which influenced him to write to the Supreme Council for the Ancient and Accepted Rite of the Northern Masonic Jurisdiction of America on 26 October 1845. Again the reader must be referred to Jackson's *Rose Croix* for the full story, but the outcome of his approach was that in the following spring he was sent a patent as Sovereign Grand Commmander of a Supreme Council for England which, curiously enough, was given the effective date of his letter of several months before.

The Supreme Council

The new Supreme Council held its first assembly on 1 December 1846 and, after meeting in the 33rd, 32nd and 31st degrees in succession to admit candidates, took two days' rest, thereafter convening a Grand College of Knights Kadosh for a like purpose. Now Kadosh was the 30th of a series of thirty-three degrees of the Ancient and Accepted Rite (the 'Scottish' Rite in America and elsewhere); the 18th was, of course, that of Rose Croix: both offered, as we have but recently observed, cherished opportunities for a Knight Templar to advance within his own encampment.

There were, in the reviving Grand Conclave (according to Jackson), several who were also active in the business of the Supreme Council and so there was probably a measure of agreement on the principle of rationalization; the practice was another matter. Ahead lay the difficult task of persuading the encampments themselves to yield to the new body their inherent rights in the Rose Croix, Kadosh and Ne Plus Ultra degrees and then to petition from it warrants for chapters in which they could, at least, continue to work the Rose Croix. But they could not expect to be able to keep up the Kadosh because as the 30th degree of the Ancient and Accepted Rite it was now out of their reach until the chair of a Rose Croix chapter had been passed.

As to the Ne Plus Ultra, it seems to have been, and still is, something of an enigma. Even Jackson, who stands firm on so much, presents it in some of his pages as a synonym for the Rose Croix degree and on another as an alternative title for Kadosh. *Ne plus ultra* can be construed as 'nothing more beyond' and was perhaps intended in a masonic context to indicate that the summit of a rite had been achieved, or the zenith of a piece of ritual (as in the 30th degree), or – in the case of the Rose Croix – that, perfection having been reached, there is nowhere else to go. Again we must be grateful to Bridge's collection of papers; he copied in full from a manuscript book of 1830, belonging originally to Alexander Dalziel of the Royal Kent Encampment at Newcastle-upon-Tyne, what must have been the rituals there in use at that time. Bridge admits in his preface to the transcript that it contains the only ritual of the Ne Plus Ultra that he had found. It is that of a fairly short ceremony, which includes readings from the Old and New Testaments, a triangular grouping in threes of those present (an echo of Royal Arch practice), and finally the forming of a chain (which in no way resembles that in a certain part of today's Rose Croix ritual).

After that digression to examine briefly what it was that Knight Templar encampments were being expected by the new Supreme Council to stop doing, we must now see what actually happened. A glance at an early list of Rose Croix chapters indicates that Templar encampments did not form a queue for the privileges on offer. In seeking Rose Croix warrants, Mount Calvary appears to have been first off the mark in 1848; Royal Kent at Newcastle and Royal Naval at Portsmouth accepted Rose Croix warrants in 1858. The rather special arrangements for Baldwyn at Bristol are described at Appendix E. Other encampments carried on for years in the old way, issuing certificates covering the 'Rosae Crucis and Ne Plus Ultra' to the Knights Templar as they took those further steps. To cater for the deeply entrenched, 'A Lewis' (the pseudonym under which countless rituals and other masonic books have been published; now 'Lewis Masonic') was still producing in 1884 *The Perfect Ceremonies of the Masonic Knights Templar, Knight of Malta, Mediterranean Pass and Rose Croix de Heredom Degrees*. In due course, however, all was resolved and it would now be difficult to imagine English Freemasonry without 'Rose Croix and K.T.' as separate authorities, operating from two different buildings.

While many distinguished and influential Freemasons have since those days been eminent in the hierarchies of both Orders, it was in 1877 that one man, Lord Skelmersdale (who later became the Earl of Lathom), succeeded to the highest office in each and occupied them for some twenty years. That piece of history has now been repeated for in 1982 Harold Devereux Still, who had been installed as our Most Eminent and Supreme Grand Master in 1976, became

Sovereign Grand Commander, *primus inter pares*, in the Supreme Council 33°.

[1] We must not fall into the trap of calling them 'side' degrees, for this term properly describes taking a brother *aside* and communicating to him, man to man, secrets belonging to a degree not at the time under authoritative control. That of Secret Monitor was, for example, disseminated in this way before a Grand Council was brought into being.

[2] Brigadier A.C.F. Jackson's *Rose Croix* (1980, but now in a second edition) is essential reading. Emphasis has been given to the Templar nature of the Kadosh degree because it is now usual, at meetings of the 30th degree (Knight Kadosh) of the Ancient and Accepted Rite, to dilate upon this very point.

7

THE GRAND CONCLAVE, 1846-1872

Colonel Charles Kemeys Kemeys Tynte

RETURNING FROM OUR diversion, we can resume a chronological sequence with John Burckhardt's nomination and installation of Colonel Kemeys Tynte as Grand Master in 1846. The new ruler had, since 1820, governed the Craft and the Royal Arch in the Province of Somerset, and was to do so until his death in 1860. He was also in the English branch of Palaprat's non-masonic Order of the Temple, which is said to have existed until the middle of the 19th century and, as has been mentioned elsewhere, included the Duke of Sussex and many other eminent freemasons among its membership. There is in the archives of Great Priory Kemeys Tynte's hand-written register of masonic encampments, started in 1846 but, alas, he must have been too busy to keep it going after the following year. It is nonetheless a useful, if limited, source of information about defunct and existing encampments and about the contemporary members.

The pages for Baldwyn are blank because at this time it was independent of the Grand Conclave, but those for the 'Chapter of Observance' (of the Seven Degrees) in London show that Kemeys Tynte himself was installed as a knight on 15 March 1818, probably at the hands of Burckhardt who is at the head of the surviving members listed in 1846. As Tynte (which is how he enters himself in the register) is shown as residing at Bridgwater, it is not surprising to find him as one of the first joining members in 1844 of Holy Cross Encampment at Axminster, which later moved to Plymouth and faded out by 1893.

The new Grand Master appointed as his Deputy, William Stuart — also of Observance — who was to succeed him in 1861. About thirty encampments were constituted during his reign, the majority still in existence although some of these now hold Canadian or Australian warrants.

There was a good deal of administrative activity during the period, including the issue of revised editions of the *Statutes* in 1846 and 1853. A move was made towards a standardized Templar ritual, and a draft which was circulated to encampments in 1851 gained general approval; many manuscript copies exist. (Some years later similar action was taken for the Malta degree.) Also in 1851 was begun the establishment of Provincial Commanderies, generally following the boundaries already in use by the Craft and Royal Arch. In some instances, rather hopefully, Provinces were formed before there were encampments for them to comprehend!

At the end of the reign of Kemeys Tynte an interesting addition to the register was a travelling military encampment, Excelsior, warranted in 1860 for the 21st Regiment of Foot (the Royal North British [Scots] Fusiliers), who were at the time stationed in Barbados. As with the ambulatory Craft lodges of the day, the postings hither and thither of the commissioned officers who for the most part constituted its membership made it difficult to keep it going. In 1886 the last surviving knightly fusilier returned the charter to Grand Conclave.

That Kemeys Tynte earned the respect and affection of his brother knights can be seen from the fact that, during his lifetime, encampments were named after him. One, after amalgamation, continues within the United Preceptory of Kemeys Tynte and Temple Cressing No. 45 of London.

William Stuart

On the death of Kemeys Tynte in November 1860, William Stuart acted as Grand Master until, duly elected, he was installed in that office in January 1861. Bridge, whose notes and records have been so helpful in preparing this book, has very little to tell us about this Grand Master. From Kemeys Tynte's short-lived register we know him to have joined the Chapter of Observance on 16 January 1834. He is shown simply as 'Esquire', residing at Aldenham Abbey, near Watford. It is thus appropriate that he became a founder and the first Commander in 1840 of the Watford Encampment; this subsequently took his name and is today the Stuart Preceptory No 28. But we do not know where and when he was installed as a Knight Templar.

We do know, however, that he was the son of an Irish Archbishop and was a Member of Parliament, and was in 1833 appointed Senior Grand Warden in the United Grand Lodge, and it is from this record that we find the date of his death — 1874.

During his Grand Mastership of some eleven years about fifty encampments were added to the roll, a high proportion of them overseas. The establishment of the Orders abroad was to some extent accelerated by the grant of powers to colonial Provincial Commanders to issue dispensations to petitioners; thereby they were enabled to form and operate their encampments while the warrants therefor were being drawn up, signed and sealed and conveyed by whatever means were available to the knights concerned.

We shall be discussing in a later chapter the changes in dress for the knights of the two Orders, and this is another subject which came up during the 1860s. But there were other proposed alterations in the *Statutes* which are worthy of mention here: one, in 1864, was to dispense with the Royal Arch qualification for a candidate. That was rejected and so it is curious to find only two years later a suggestion that *either* the Royal Arch *or* the Rose Croix degree should be a prerequisite for admission. This, too, was turned down; it is scarcely surprising since, in the past, the Rose Croix had generally followed and had certainly not preceded the Templar degree. At Baldwyn and in Ireland this was, of course, and still is the case.

In 1868, five years after the final renumbering of the lodges of the English Craft, it was thought desirable to apply a comparable process to Knight Templar encampments. Thus began the enumeration which continues today.

At around this time we read of 'Conventions' separately held with the masonic Templar authorities of Scotland and Ireland. These were, in fact, tremors of a change that, as Bridge bluntly put it, 'nearly wrecked the Order'. The idea of a Convent General was being discussed, mostly *in camera*, but that vexed and vexing subject must be left to chapter 9.

8

IRELAND AND SCOTLAND TO 1872

Our brother knights in Ireland figured prominently in the gestation, birth, life and unlamented end of the Convent General, and those of Scotland were 'marginally' involved. Before we tell that tale we should therefore, and as succinctly as we may, bring them up to the starting line at which, for England, we already stand.

IRELAND

The Early Grand Encampment

In chapter 3 we touched briefly upon the Early Grand Encampment and we must now consider the most likely date for its constitution. *The Rules of the High Knights Templars* of 1788 gave us a date of 1765 for the knighthood of the senior member, and thereby the earliest recorded date for the conferment of the Templar degree in Ireland. And those *Rules* also include the information that the Early Grand Encampment had been *revived* on 26 September 1786, but for how long had it then been in suspended animation? *The Irish Freemasons' Calendar and Directory* (annual) claims at the head of the relevant section that the Order of the Temple dates from '*ante* AD1770'. One would have hoped to find in the writings of Sir Charles Cameron (for instance in his excellent paper about the chivalric Orders in *AQC* 13, 1900) something definitive on this point, because Sir Charles was at the time Great Seneschal and Deputy Grand Master of the Irish Great Priory, but he confesses that he has been unable to find a date.

Nevertheless it may fairly be inferred that the first governing authority for the Order in Ireland came into being a few years before Dunckerley's Grand Conclave for England. Unlike the latter, and although it seems to have issued some sixty warrants (including one for an encampment at Scarborough in Yorkshire), it was not to be long-lasting. Its last surviving record, for St. John the Baptist's day 1826, was of its renunciation of rights over its encampments in Scotland and by 1837 it had been replaced by the Supreme Grand Encampment.

The Kilwinning Grand Chapter

It was also in chapter 3 that we introduced the 'High Knight Templars of Ireland Kilwinning Lodge' of 1779. By 1803 this was known as the Grand Kilwinning Chapter and it soon afterwards began to issue warrants for 'chapters and encampments of High Knights Templars', claiming in those documents 'special authority from the Mother Lodge of Kilwinning, Scotland'. It is said that its action arose from a resolution in 1805 by the Irish Craft Grand Lodge to take the Order of the Temple under its own control and to issue charters accordingly. A storm of protest arose from all the then existing bodies, supreme and subordinate, and Grand Lodge went no further in the matter.

The Supreme Grand Encampment

In 1823 there was a proposal, engendered no doubt by royal interest in the Order in England, to form an overall authority for Knights Templar in Ireland with a nobleman as Grand Master. It took some years for the scheme to reach fruition for it was not until 1837 that the first convocation of the Supreme Grand Encampment was held, when Augustus Frederick, the 3rd Duke of Leinster (who had been Grand Master of the Irish Craft since 1813 and the Sovereign Grand Commander of the Supreme Council since its constitution in 1824) assumed the throne and retained it (and the other exalted offices) until his death in 1874.

Although we cannot here deal with the history of their introduction, it must here be observed that the Irish Supreme Grand Encampment, and the Irish Great Priory which it later became, had under control not only 'High Knights Templars and Masonic Knights of Malta' but also the 'Councils of the preceding degrees of Knights of the Sword, Knights of the East and Knights of the East and West, commonly called Red Cross Masons' which were held under Templar warrants. We shall have occasion to mention these Red Cross degrees later on but for the moment we must turn our attention to Scotland.

SCOTLAND

The Royal Grand Conclave

In 1809 began the first movement in Scotland towards the formation of a sovereign Knight Templar authority. Alexander Deuchar, another of those names which echo in masonic history, was the leader and it was soon decided to seek the blessing of the Duke of Kent, Royal Grand Patron of the Grand Conclave in London. There was correspondence with Waller Rodwell Wright, the English Grand Master, and the Duke signed a 'Charter of Dispensation' appointing Deuchar as the Scottish Grand Master. Understandably the Duke wanted the new body to follow so far as it could the rules agreed for England.

After many preliminary meetings, the Grand Conclave was consecrated in 1811 and was seen to have under its banners several of the encampments formerly under the Irish Early Grand Encampment, together with some which had been working under Craft or Royal Arch warrants and a few which had been constituted since the Duke of Kent's authority came into force.

George Draffen's *Pour la Foy* (1949) well describes the ups and downs of the Scottish Grand Conclave during the following decades but we must refer to one quite extraordinary proposal of 1844, to allow *non-masons* to be admitted to the Order. They were to pay ten guineas upon their reception, while Master Masons would be charged seven and Royal Arch Masons only four. Although this provision was agreed, it seems but infrequently to have been brought into use. In 1848, the Duke of Leeds — not a freemason — was created a Knight Templar in Great Priory and was only a few months later elected Seneschal, an office which he held until 1857. The Bishop of Edinburgh (presumably of the Episcopal Church) is said to have been similarly admitted. But in 1856 all former Statutes were abrogated and the new rules then brought in included one requiring that all future candidates should be members of the Royal Arch degree.

There was an interesting example of Scottish 'expansion' into England in 1847, when 'The Priory of the Temple in London' was chartered on 11 March and was given the number 13 on the roll. It was recorded as dormant in 1855 and, although in 1861 an application was made to 'repone' (the Scottish equivalent of 'revive') it, Edinburgh wisely refused it.

By this time the governing body of the Royal Grand Conclave was variously known as the Chapter General or as the *Grand* Priory but the one Minute-book was used, regardless of the title favoured on a particular occasion. (Much later, in 1896 at the annual tripartite conference with the emancipated English and Irish Great Priories, it was the Chapter General of Scotland who participated.)

The Early Grand Encampment

It may be recalled that in chapter 3 was mentioned the role of Ireland in establishing the first Knight Templar encampments in Scotland. Despite the appearance of the Scottish Grand Conclave under its Royal Grand Patron, and the adherence of some of the Irish encampments to the new authority, Ireland issued further warrants, the last in 1826, not long before Dublin renounced its control over its Scottish offspring. At the same time it gave a patent to Frater Robert Martin (who had been acting for a while as a kind of 'Provincial Prior') constituting him the first Grand Master of the Early Grand Encampment of Scotland. He retained that office until his death in 1857, ruling over a group of fiercely independent 'Early Granders' who wanted nothing to do with the Deuchar interlopers!

The Great Priory

Not surprisingly, the Royal Grand Conclave, the Grand Priory or the Chapter General regarded the Early Grand Encampment as irregular and it was not until 1909, and after prolonged negotiation, that a union was effected and then not to the satisfaction of all the knights. From this moment onwards the title of Great Priory came into use.

We are, however, racing too far ahead of events in England and Ireland in which Scotland was at first also involved; of these the next chapter will tell.

9

CONVENT GENERAL 1872-1895

We who, in this matter, enjoy the luxury of hindsight may yet wonder how this untypical and quite extraordinary interlude in the history of our United Orders could have been allowed to proceed past the exploratory stage. But we are about to describe events which were set in train well over a century ago and, even though we may not understand the views of some of the brother knights of the day, we must report on decisions then made which created deep divisions among the membership.

The Preliminaries

It is by no means clear as to how and where it all began, and to whom may be ascribed the spark which began it, but in the years 1867 and 1868 there were 'talks about talks' between 'plenipotentiaries' of the Grand Masters of England, Ireland and Scotland. Documents then signed looked ahead to closer co-operation, to the 'interchange of courtesy and hospitality' and to concluding an agreement as to the intended formation of the Convent General under whose oversight the three hitherto independent Templar authorities would in future operate. The representative of William Stuart, the Grand Master of England, in all these activities was Sir Patrick MacChombaich de Colquhoun, his Grand Chancellor and a Queen's Counsel, who was later regarded as having laboured 'not wisely but too well'.

Scotland, although they had figured in the preliminary discussions, sensibly withdrew before they had committed themselves too far, but England and Ireland carried on with the scheme and produced a draft for new Statutes which, as Bridge puts it 'were rushed through Grand Conclave [of England] in a manner that can only be described as improper'.

The Repercussions

We cannot do better than continue to quote from G. E. W. Bridge's notes on the events immediately following:

> When the Provinces and Encampments had had time to realize the extent of the changes (presented to them as a *fait accompli*), they combined and fought them tooth and nail, and the headquarters was [after a couple of years had been allowed for a sort of 'trial run'] flooded with 'Respectful Memorials' (and others less respectful) from all Provinces and from encampments ranging from Australia and China, throughout England, to the West Indies – all couched in similar terms.

A typical example, addressed in 1874 to the Very High and Eminent National Great Prior, is from 'the Sir Knights of the Province of Devon in Provincial Priory assembled' and a printed copy, with its covering letter, would appear to have been sent to every English preceptory. Thus were fanned the flames of revolution!

In summarizing the objections thus raised, we are able to indicate the changes which the new Convent General was committed to enforce:

1. The omission of the word 'Masonic' from the title of the Order; this was seen as putting it once more at risk under the Unlawful Societies Act of 1799.
2. The claim that the masonic Order derived from the medieval knightly Orders.
3. The changes of nomenclature: 'encampment' to 'preceptory', 'Commander' to 'Preceptor', and so on.
4. The abolition of 'Past Rank', which meant that a Great or Provincial Officer had to revert to the status of Past Preceptor, or even that of Brother Knight, when his term of office expired. This highly unpopular alteration to the rules made it necessary for those affected to adjust their regalia to the higher rank for perhaps one year only and then to have to remove the trimmings!
5. The creation of Knights Grand Cross and Knights Commander in both England and Ireland was to be at the discretion of the Grand Master of the Convent General (and not of the Great Priors – which was now to be their title – for each country).
6. The concentration of all executive power in the hands of a relatively small number of officers of the Convent General in London.
7. The failure to give adequate warning to all that the new Constitution was to be presented, passed and put into operation at a meeting of Grand Conclave on 13 December 1872. There should have been ample opportunity for consideration in the Provinces, and for full discussion thereafter before the proposals were so hastily put to the vote.

Nevertheless . . .

Despite the immediate outcry and that which was to continue for some years to come the Convent General was established. The first step, so far as England was concerned, was the resignation of William Stuart from the Grand Mastership. The Reverend John Huyshe of Devonshire, the Deputy Grand Master, acted in his stead until 7 April 1873 when H.R.H. Albert Edward, Prince of Wales (who had first displayed an interest in the Orders by his presence at Grand Conclave in May 1870, when he stayed to witness the Malta ceremony), having been nominated and elected at the controversial meeting in the previous December, was at the age of 31 installed as the Grand Master of the Convent General 'of England and Wales, and Ireland'. His election in Dublin had taken place on 15 January, where it is to be supposed that the changes were similarly unpopular. The Earl of Limerick, who was also an English baron, was appointed National Great Prior of England and the Duke of Leinster, who had served independently as Grand Master since 1837, was placed in charge of the National Great Priory of Ireland. These cumbersome new titles were usually reflected in the offices which now had to be filled and even more awful – in the view of many – was the creation for the superior organization of such ranks as 'Arch Chancellor' and 'Arch Registrar'. Less official but very probably used in conversation was the term 'arch villain' for Colquhoun, who was blamed (rightly or wrongly) for all that was happening to the Orders.

Something Positive

Set out in the agenda for the meeting of Convent General on 9 May 1873 were proposed rules for the clothing of Knights Templar and Knights of Malta. The mantles and tunics there prescribed are those which we wear today. Gone were the aprons and other details of former days, although – obviously after strong representations from the rank and file – there was in 1875 a modification permitting those installed as knights before Convent General was established to wear their old costume.

Out in the field the expansion of the English United Orders could be seen to have slowed down. Of the thirty-six preceptories warranted during the life of the Convent General no less than sixteen were for overseas where the rumblings from London were scarcely audible. Lord Limerick resigned in 1876 and his successor, the Earl of Shrewsbury died five months after installation. But then to the office of Great Prior came Lord Skelmersdale, later to become the Earl of Lathom.

The Earl of Lathom

Here is another of those great freemasons whose names echo in our halls of fame, and whose face is familiar to many of us from his portrait at Mark Masons' Hall. We have earlier mentioned that he was the Sovereign Grand Commander of the Ancient and Accepted Rite from 1877 until his death in 1898, and that he was our Great Prior from 1877 until the Convent General had run its course. We can now add that he ruled the Grand Lodge of Mark Master Masons for twenty years from 1878 and that in 1891 he added to these three eminent offices that of Pro Grand Master of the Craft.

It is not unreasonable to suppose that the high regard in which Lord Lathom was held, and his careful and tactful discharge of the duties which fell to him in the United Orders, played no small part in holding together a masonic organization which was at times rather near boiling-point.

Plodding Along

Although it was possible during the period to bring before the National Great Priory, with proper debate, a number of amendments to the unwelcome Constitutions, the cumbersome machinery of the Convent General delayed their statutory confirmation. This procedure entailed asking Ireland whether they would approve of what England proposed, and *vice versa*, with the outcome not necessarily a foregone conclusion!

It would be as well to consider how the Convent General conducted its business. In the archives are two weighty tomes – its Attendance (signature) Book and its Minute Book (in the event much slimmer volumes would have proved more than adequate!), and from these we find that the Convent General was summoned on only nine occasions during its twenty-three years' existence.

7 April 1873 – at Willis's Rooms, King Street, St. James's.
This was for the purpose of installing the Prince of Wales as Grand Master and was the only meeting for which a large number of signatures appear. Huyshe, the Acting Grand Master of Grand Conclave, presided until he had placed the Prince on the throne.

9 May 1873 – at the City Terminus Hotel, Cannon Street.
The Earl of Limerick, National Great Prior of England, took the chair in the absence of the Grand Master (who attended no more meetings of the Convent General). Only four names appear in the Attendance Book but the Minutes show that fifty voted on a resolution!.
30 October 1874 – at Freemasons' Hall, Dublin.
Townshend, the Arch Chancellor (an Irish knight) presided.
29 October 1875 – at the City Terminus Hotel.
Lord Limerick was in the chair and Colquhoun signed in as Great Registrar (but could still have been Arch Registrar).
27 October 1876 – at Dublin.
Townshend presided but it is interesting to see that on this occasion Colquhoun appeared as Preceptor of Faith and Fidelity No.26; he was no doubt in the process of resigning from his 'Arch' office.
8 December 1876 – at the City Terminus Hotel.
Lord Shrewsbury took the chair: Colquhoun did not sign in.
18 April 1890 – over thirteen years since the previous meeting! Shadwell Clerke, the Great Sub-Prior, presided. Sixteen signed in but, of course, there could have been more present.
9 May 1890 – at Mark Mason's Hall, Great Queen Street.
This time a gap of only twenty-one days between meetings. Shadwell Clerke again stood in for the Grand Master.
11 May 1894 – at Mark Masons' Hall.
The Earl of Euston, National Sub-Prior, took the chair. This was the last gathering of the Convent General.

Whether or not any of these dates coincided with meetings of the respective National Great Priories, it is clear that the Convent General was being run, in effect, by some kind of central 'executive' who were making the decisions, usually without benefit of ratification. There was, of course, a great deal of correspondence but democracy was conspicuous by its absence.

An Unwanted Ritual

A noteworthy nonsense of the 1870s was the production by the Convent General of an official ritual, based on the report of a Commission which included the plenipotentiaries previously mentioned. Colquhoun signs this document as Arch Registrar and his Irish counterpart as Arch Chancellor, and seven other members added their names. It is interesting to read the addendum, signed by the redoubtable Shadwell Clerke as Provincial Prior of Sussex and as Sub-Prior for England and Wales (a few years later he became the Grand Secretary of the Craft):

> I regret that I am unable to concur in this Report, or to give my approval to the Draft of New Ritual submitted by the other Members of the Commission.

The ritual was made obligatory in 1878 but was wholly ignored by both England (especially Baldwyn) and Ireland. Curiously enough, Canada adopted it!

Canada's brief entry into the story deserves some explanation. Up to 1868, the Provincial Grand Commandery there had overseen the English encampments which, from 1824 onwards, had been constituted in the country. A request for sovereign status in 1868 received only a limited response; the Provincial ruler, Colonel W. J. Macleod Moore was given the local rank of Grand Prior for Canada and was allowed to retain some of the dues which had previously been transmitted to London. Seven years later, however, independence was granted and the Canadian preceptories (as they were now styled) were transferred to their own Great Priory. Perhaps partly as a gesture of gratitude, this new authority had between 1876 and 1884 voluntarily adhered to the Convent General, although it had been allowed to retain some measure of autonomy. In 1884 the Canadian knights were 'absolved from their allegiance to the Grand Master of the United Kingdom' and the Sovereign Great Priory of Canada of today was established, with Macleod Moore as Grand Master *ad vitam.* (His is yet another of those names writ large in masonic history but the reader will have to look elsewhere for his story.)

The End of the Convent General

From about 1889, it was clear that rot was setting in at all levels. The restrictive rules had discouraged preceptories to the extent that some had ceased to meet regularly; others tried to hang on with minimal attendances, reluctant to surrender their warrants. Sadly, because of inability to settle their arrears, fifteen were removed from the roll in 1888.

Convent General then attempted to ease some of the rules but were frustrated by the creaking of their own machinery. The National Great Priory of England achieved changes on a grand scale, including the restoration of Past Rank. But these concessions were too late. It had become abundantly clear that the Convent General's demise was long overdue.

A Commission composed of seven each from the English and Irish National Great Priories was charged in May 1894 with the tasks of discovering what had gone wrong and of devising a way out. Its report was laid before the English Great Priory one year later and was printed in its *Calendar for 1895–1896*. It will have given rise to many dour remarks about why it had taken twenty years for most of the points made in the 'memorials' to be included in an official document. It acknowledged that, from the very start, the absence of Scotland from the 'union' had diminished any chance of success that it might otherwise have had and scathingly observed that Canada's later withdrawal from its temporary attachment had come about when they had found that 'the Convent General was merely a figure of speech'. There were many other uncomplimentary aspects of what was a lengthy document but the commission urged that 'the excellent objects which it was hoped would be effected [by the Convent General] should by no means be abandoned'.

To this end they proposed 'that Ireland be invited to enter into a new Convention, into which it is hoped Scotland may also enter, which, while giving each National Great Body the entire control of its own affairs, will unite the Order in the United Kingdom under one Head'.

Ireland adopted the report in every particular and there was discussion with Scotland. One of the welcome recommendations related to the creation of Knights Grand Cross, an honour which seemed recently to have been rather generously conferred. (In December 1893 eight were so invested, together with no fewer than fourteen Knights Commander, but this could possibly have been a 'catching-up' process!) Other than royal personages, no more than fifteen of the higher distinction were to exist in England and nine each in Ireland and Scotland, and these limitations have been observed ever since.

We need not here go into the detailed arrangements which followed the acceptance of the report. The Grand Master, the Prince of Wales, gave his blessing and on 19 July 1895, he applied his signature to a beautifully engrossed Declaration (the text of which is reproduced at Appendix D). The Convent General took its last shuddering breath, England and Ireland once more became independent of each other and His Royal Highness acceded to the request that he should henceforth be addressed as 'The Sovereign of the Order in the United Kingdom'. Under his benevolent oversight England, Ireland and Scotland were in complete harmony.

10

GREAT PRIORY 1895-1991

THE STORY OF our first hundred years has logically and conveniently spread itself over several chapters, partly because of its length and partly because of certain changes of direction. With the end of the Convent General, however, the United Orders in England were able to set in train and enjoy the steady and peaceful progress which it is now our responsibility to continue into our third century. Neither G. E. W. Bridge nor R. M. Handfield-Jones, to whom (among others) we are indebted for the maintenance and organization of such records as we have, has been able to find much happening that has been out of the ordinary between 1895 and their day, and the succeeding years have been similarly devoid of the unusual. But we have had, as was the case in the earlier period, some great freemasons to rule over us, and the knights of today may like to know something about them while, here and there, we report on events which rose above the level of routine.

The Prince of Wales

The masonic career of H.R.H. Albert Edward, Prince of Wales, ought perhaps to have been set down in the previous chapter but as, with the beginning of this one, he takes up a supreme office in the United Orders, we may be forgiven for the delay.

Like other royal freemasons who have figured in this book, the Prince was initiated abroad. It was in Stockholm in 1868 that he was admitted to the *Nordiska Första* Lodge of St. John at the hands of Prince Oscar, soon to be King of Sweden. He was at once passed through the ten degrees of the Scandinavian Rite. In the following year he was appointed Past Grand Master in the United Grand Lodge of England and only five years later was enthroned as Grand Master, and as First Grand Principal in the Royal Arch, in succession to the Marquess of Ripon. Also in 1874 he was advanced to the 33rd degree in the Ancient and Accepted Rite. In 1886 he became Grand Master of the Mark Grand Lodge. He continued to rule over the Craft, Royal Arch and Mark until he ascended the throne as King Edward VII in 1901.

The Prince, as we have already noted, was present at Grand Conclave in May 1870 and stayed for the Malta ceremony. It could be that his membership of the higher degrees in Sweden was regarded as having qualified him to attend, or perhaps he had been admitted to the two degrees 'at sight' or at a private meeting convened by the Grand Master, William Stuart. When he was installed in 1873 as Grand Master of the Convent General it was his first 'active' masonic office, although those in the Craft and Royal Arch would soon follow.

In 1863 at the Ball given by the Apollo University Lodge of Oxford (*see* Plate 12), the Prince of Wales and his young bride, Princess Alexandra, were received under an arch of steel which can only have been formed by knights of the Coeur de Lion Encampment. As he surveyed all the Craft and Templar regalia around him, one wonders whether he could then have imagined the role which was to be his in the years to come.

He ruled as Sovereign of the United Orders in England, Scotland and Ireland from 1895 until 1901, and thereafter became Royal Grand Patron. His death in 1910 ended forty years of service as a Knight Templar. It is worth mentioning that he had in 1881 been appointed Bailiff Grand Cross of the Sovereign Order of Malta and that in 1888 he became Grand Prior of the Order of St. John and was thus probably unique in concurrently holding high rank in three Orders derived from the Hospitallers.

The Earl of Euston

Henry James Fitzroy, Earl of Euston, was elected and installed as Grand Master on 8 May 1896. He was the eldest son of the 7th Duke of Grafton but predeceased his father, who lived to the patriarchal age of 97. Lord Euston was of royal descent because the first Duke had been the son of King Charles II and the Duchess of Cleveland.

His masonic responsibilities ranged widely. In 1887, at the age of 39, he was appointed Provincial Grand Master, and in the following year Royal Arch Grand Superintendent of Northamptonshire and Huntingdonshire. In 1894 he also took over the Mark Province (which included Bedfordshire), and also the Mark Province of

Leicestershire and Rutland, having become Pro Grand Master in the Mark some months previously. He had already been enthroned, in 1889, 1892 and 1893 respectively, as the ruler of the Royal and Select Masters, the Order of the Red Cross of Constantine and the Allied Degrees and in the Ancient and Accepted Rite he joined the Supreme Council in 1895. In all these offices he continued until his death at the age of 64 in 1912.

In the United Orders, however, he resigned from the highest office in 1907 to facilitate the election of the Duke of Connaught who at once asked him to be his Pro Grand Master. He spared no effort in carrying out all his duties and it was said of him at his passing that he would be remembered 'for his kindness, genial presence, his broad and politic view of all matters submitted to him' and that he 'was a firm friend, a faithful brother mason and a true gentleman'.

Conferences and Concordats

It was during Lord Euston's Grand Mastership that England, Ireland and Scotland agreed to hold annual meetings to discuss questions of mutual concern and also agreed that henceforth each Great Priory would be free to pursue its own course. These have continued to the present day, usually held alternately in London, Dublin and Edinburgh.

In 1905 a deputation headed by the Grand Master attended the Triennial Convention of the Grand Encampment of the United States. (This event will be referred to again in chapter 16.) The visit led to a Concordat and in 1907 both the United States and Canada were represented at the annual conference of the United Orders. On subsequent occasions similar visits have been exchanged and it is always a pleasure to welcome our brother knights from America both at Great Priory and in our preceptories.

The Duke of Connaught

H.R.H. Arthur, Duke of Connaught and Strathearn, who had ruled the United Orders in Ireland since 1878, and had long held office as Provincial Prior for Sussex, was in 1907 invited to become the Sovereign of the Orders of the Temple and Malta in the United Kingdom. He was also elected Grand Master of England in succession to the Earl of Euston. He had been Grand Master of the

English Craft, First Grand Principal in the Royal Arch and Grand Master of the Mark since 1901, and had been a member of the 33rd degree of the Ancient and Accepted Rite since 1878.

In December 1918 the Orders gave thanks for the ending of the first world war, very appropriately, in Temple Church, London, and the sermon was given by the Master of the Temple. Great Priory created a precedent in 1922 by convening in the Chapter House at Durham Cathedral and by attending, with all the knights in the habit of the Order, a service in the splendid cathedral. In 1928 a meeting was similarly held at Liverpool.

The Duke of Connaught's long and devoted service to Freemasonry in general is so well known that it needs little elaboration here, but he must have derived especial pleasure from the consecration and dedication in 1933 of the new Freemasons' Hall in Great Queen Street. His retirement in 1939 from all high masonic offices at the age of 89 marked the end of an era and his passing in 1942 was widely mourned.

Pro Grand Masters

On the death of the Earl of Euston, Richard Loveland Loveland, the Great Seneschal, was appointed Pro Grand Master. He was succeeded in 1920 by Major-General Thomas Pleydell Calley, on whose death in 1932 the Earl of Harewood took office.

The Earl of Harewood

Henry George Charles Lascelles, 6th Earl of Harewood, was — on the resignation of the Duke of Connaught in 1939 — elected and installed as Grand Master. The husband of Princess Mary, the Princess Royal, he too gave service in a wider masonic field — as the head of the Craft and Royal Arch from 1942, as the Provincial Grand Master for West Yorkshire in the Mark from 1929, as the Grand Supreme Ruler in the Order of the Secret Monitor from 1932 to 1936 and as a member of the 33rd degree from 1936. His passing in 1947 was keenly felt throughout English Freemasonry.

Lord Harris

George St. Vincent, 5th Lord Harris, the Great Seneschal, was elected and installed in 1947 in succession to Lord Harewood and was Grand Master of the United Orders for over twenty-five years.

Like so many of his predecessors he was a dedicated freemason; he was the Junior Grand Warden of the Craft and the Grand Scribe Nehemiah in the Royal Arch in 1927, and became Grand Master of the Mark in 1954, and also served as Inspector General for Kent in the Ancient and Accepted Rite. He was held in great affection by all and there were many expressions of regret when advancing years decided him to retire in 1973. Until his death in 1984 he maintained an unfailing interest in the United Orders and sent many kindly messages through his successor to the knights at our annual communications.

A memorable event during his reign was the convocation of Great Priory at York in 1957, which was followed by a service in the Minster (*see* plate 20).

Lieutenant-Colonel John Leicester-Warren

It was again to the Great Seneschal whom we looked for a successor to Lord Harris and Lt.-Col. John Leighton Byrne Leicester-Warren was elected and installed on 16 May 1973. He was Provincial Grand Master for Cheshire in the Mark and was a Member of the Supreme Council of the Ancient and Accepted Rite. Sadly his tenure of the Grand Mastership was all too short for he died on 10 August 1975.

Harold Devereux Still

The Very Eminent Knight Harold Still, Great Seneschal, acted as Grand Master until his election and installation as such on 19 May 1976. High in the councils of almost every Order and degree within English Freemasonry, he brought a wealth of experience to his office and has ruled wisely and well, earning the acclaim of every knight in the Orders and the affection of those who have been so fortunate as to meet him.

We have mentioned elsewhere his place at the head of the Ancient and Accepted Rite and it is a peculiarly happy circumstance that the Orders of the Temple and the Rose Croix, which were at the commencement of our story so closely related, are again so nearly linked.

A most significant change, early in his reign, was that the word 'Masonic' was restored to the full title of our Orders. It may be recalled that its deletion, when the Convent General was created in

1872, was a matter which aroused much unfavourable comment. Once again we gratefully became 'the United Religious, Military and Masonic Orders', with our status clearly defined.

Banners and Pennons

Also among the alterations were some relating to clothing, arms and insignia, perhaps the most interesting to the knights of today being the withdrawal of the privilege enjoyed by our forebears of carrying a pennon!

There continued until the 1972 *Statutes* the provision that, optionally, a knight could bear a swallow-tailed pennon of red and white in the proportions of the ribbon of the Order. Preceptors and knights above that grade were entitled to carry a banner, of 26 inches by 30 inches, 'Argent, a Cross Patee gules, charged with the personal device of the knight'. It was this provision which was revoked in 1976.

One reads in the archives and in the Minutes of half a century or more ago of what must have been quite colourful scenes in Great Priory, and also within preceptories. There was a recommendation in 1897, for instance, that every preceptory's banner should be brought or sent to Great Priory convocations and there displayed. It is recorded in the early 1900s that when a Provincial Prior, newly appointed, came to pay homage to the Grand Master he was introduced to the sound of trumpets and was preceded into Great Priory by his Provincial Sword Bearer and Banner Bearer. From a paper written by A. J. Collins for the fiftieth anniversary of King Edward VII Preceptory No. 173 it is learned that in the 1920s its Past Preceptors certainly provided themselves with banners. Its meetings took place on the eve of Great Priory and in the temple which was already laid out for the following day, with the banners of many distinguished knights already in place, as well as the standards of numerous preceptories adorning the walls. The membership of King Edward VII included trumpeters and their services were in demand for Chapters of Great Priory for the fanfares which are now the responsibility of the Great Organist!

Overseas Visits

In 1977 a most extensive tour was undertaken by the Grand Master and the Great Marshal, Brigadier Geoffrey Galloway, which comprehended Sri Lanka, Singapore, Hong Kong, New Zealand

and every Province of Australia. The report thereon made fascinating reading and the Grand Master was, as he put it, 'made aware of the great strength of the bonds of the Order'. Those bonds were not weakened when, in more recent years, the Provincial Priories in Australasia became sovereign jurisdictions.

The Christian Orders and the Church

In an era when so much has been implied about Freemasonry and imputed to freemasons, and in particular that the Craft and Christianity are incompatible, it is something of a relief to be able to record that Great Priory has been able to follow the precedents set in the 1920s under the Duke of Connaught, and renewed under Lord Harris, by offering prayer and praise in our great cathedrals. In 1980 at Wells, in 1984 at Lincoln and in 1989 at Worcester, the Grand Master was joined by large numbers of the knights. On each occasion, the proceedings began with a special convocation of Great Priory in the Chapter House at which a most interesting paper was read. The knights then processed in full regalia into the nave for a service in which members of their families and of the general public were welcome participants. The visit to Wells was of unique significance to the Grand Master for his ancestor, Doctor John Still, had been Bishop of Bath and Wells from 1593 to 1608, and the procession into the cathedral passed the prelate's tomb at the foot of the Chapter-House stairs.

The Way Ahead

It is given to few of us to be able to see into the future. We go forward in faith, with hope of achievement, and with the charity that becomes a Christian knight. Let us not forget the past; we honour our founders and those whose courage and vision have through two centuries guided our progress. We shall need as much courage, and we must pray for as much vision, as the Templar and Malta banners lead us into the years ahead.

11

IRELAND AND SCOTLAND 1872-1991

WE HAVE TOLD as much as we may of the early history of our two sister Constitutions of Ireland and Scotland and have carried it forward to the year in which they faced decisions about their relationships with the new Convent General. It is only fair that we should now look at one or two of the more interesting events which have coloured for them the last 120 years, exploring as seems necessary the background against which those events occurred.

IRELAND

Under the Convent General

Because Ireland chose to adhere to the Convent General the reader can be referred to chapter 9 for those matters in which action was taken in parallel, so to speak, with England. The Duke of Leinster, who had to the satisfaction of all governed the Supreme Grand Encampment there for some thirty-five years, in 1873 accepted — until his passing in the following year — a less independent role as National Great Prior under the Grand Mastership of the Prince of Wales. The Duke's astonishing record of service to Irish Freemasonry had begun in 1813 when — at the age of only 22 — he was installed as Grand Master of the Craft, an office which he discharged for no less than sixty-one years. He was also, from 1824 until his death, at the head of the Ancient and Accepted Rite.

He was followed as National Great Prior by Marquess Conyngham who was in turn succeeded in 1878 by the Duke of Connaught, and the latter's term of office as Great Prior and then as Grand Master of the United Orders in Ireland continued for the remarkable period of sixty-four years.

The Order of the Red Cross

When the proposed union with England under the Convent General seemed imminent there were thoughts about the Order of the Red Cross (often described as 'the Green Degrees') and its place within the Templar/Malta organization. In 1871 a motion was discussed for transferring these degrees, which have no Christian connotation, 'to the governing bodies of the Rites to which they belong'. The proposal was rejected by fifteen votes to two, and indeed it is by no means clear as to what governing bodies then existed to accept the responsibility.

Nevertheless interest in the Red Cross Order decreased. It was rather strange that, despite the decision that had been made to keep them going, preceptory warrants from this time onwards omitted the former authority to confer the green before the 'black' degrees of the Temple and Malta.

By the turn of the century there had been a move to suppress the Red Cross altogether but there was a rally, predominantly fostered by the northern counties. But when, in 1923, it was found that the Order was being worked in only a few preceptories and in those at irregular intervals, a further proposal for its closure came before Great Priory. On this occasion there came into being a 'governing body' to take it over; a Grand Council of Knight Masons was formed by twenty-one leading members of the Great Priory, progressively reinforced by the principal officers and past rulers of the subordinate councils which came into existence.

There are now about seventy-five councils, some of them in Africa and Hong Kong where Irish Craft Freemasonry flourishes. Curiously enough, since in America the Red Cross degrees remain very actively within the Templar/Malta sphere, warrants were granted in the United States from 1936 onwards. Some years later most of these councils formed themselves into a sovereign Grand Council (the only one so far outside Ireland) but three in Ohio constitute a Province still under Dublin.

The United Orders Today

It is statistically noteworthy that the oldest surviving preceptory, the Grand Master's at Dublin, dates from 1837 and that there are currently some ninety-five on the register. Comparison with the number of seventy-five Red Cross Councils, the earliest warranted in 1924, engenders some interesting theories but they cannot be pursued here.

In Ireland, Freemasonry is stronger in the north than in the south and this is reflected in the fact that the one Templar Province, for East Ulster, comprehends some forty-seven of the total number of preceptories. Those in the north-west and those in the republic are directly ruled from Great Priory. A fairly recent year-book records seven overseas, one in New Zealand and the rest in Africa.

SCOTLAND

Recapitulation

In chapter 8, because Scotland remained independent of the Convent General, it seemed logical to intrude very briefly upon the period which this chapter is intended to cover. So let it be recalled that, while England and Ireland coped with the problems of their uneasy consortium, Scotland had a few problems of its own. Not the least was the existence in North Britain of two authorities controlling the Orders of the Temple and Malta – the Royal Grand Conclave of 1811 and the Early Grand Encampment of 1826.

England could not recognize both and had, of course, been linked with the Royal Grand Conclave from its beginnings by the Duke of Kent's dual patronage.

Divided Loyalties

It was an unhappy state of affairs, especially for those knights who, in Craft and Royal Arch settings, could mingle freely but were not allowed to work together in Christian chivalry. England became involved in print in 1901 when it was reported in Great Priory that 'a *quasi* Grand Body, styling itself "The Grand Encampment of the Temple and Malta in Scotland" was in existence. 'A brother professing to have been installed in the Order of the Temple in Aberdeen had sought to join a Yorkshire Preceptory but he had been admitted in a encampment not under the Chapter General.' Two years later 'the schismatic body' was identified as the Early Grand Encampment, but that adjective was quite wrong; the two authorities had always existed separately. The somewhat parliamentary language of the announcements concealed the fact that the Early Grand Encampment was not some upstart organization but had pursued a respectable but parallel course for some seventy-five years.

Union

Moves towards a possible amalgamation began in 1904 with an approach from the Grand Encampment, but the Chapter General turned that down. Other attempts eventually led to the Union in 1909 of the two bodies as 'The Great Priory of the Religious and Military Order of the Temple in Scotland' with the 9th Earl of Kintore as Grand Master. As such he continued in office until 1928, since when a succession of eminent Scots have ruled the United Orders.

Inter-Constitutional Relations

It had been customary for representatives at high level from the English, Irish and Scottish jurisdictions to meet together to discuss matters of mutual concern. At such a gathering in 1896 it was found that Scotland had, in addition to the dignities of Knight Grand Cross and Knight Commander, a third — of Knight Companion. It was decided that such knights should 'hold concurrent rank with preceptors in England and Ireland', but such a distinction no longer exists.

Of great importance has been the Concordat, signed in 1930 and — with revisions — still in force, which governs such matters as relationships, triennial conferences, the number of Knights Grand Cross, and basic principles for recognition.

The Scottish Orders Today

The Kalendar and Liber Ordinis Templi for 1988 lists 116 preceptories (the earliest dating from 1794). As is the case with the Scottish Craft and Royal Arch, a high proportion are overseas — fifty-four — mostly in countries in which there are Scottish lodges and chapters. Nineteen are in Africa, eighteen in Australia; the six in the Caribbean area include one in Panama City and there are two in Peru. The unusual exception is that under a District Priory in Italy are eight preceptories which, in the main, must draw their candidates from Italian Craft lodges and the Royal Arch chapters of English and American derivation which have been chartered in the country.

12
THE MASONIC ORDER OF MALTA

United Orders?

SOME WRITERS SUGGEST an incongruity in the union of the masonic Orders of the Temple and Malta under one authority. One theory put forward is that, when the possessions of the medieval Templars were transferred to the Hospitallers, a most unchristian hate was engendered among the survivors of the one for the members of the other; coexistence would have been anathema to them.

There are however obvious connections, both temporal and spiritual, which would appear to justify the close relationship that has been maintained from the earliest traceable history of masonic chivalry. The two Orders in the Holy Land gave complementary service; on occasion they fought and died side by side. While they both accumulated land and wealth, and although some of their number strayed from the path which they had vowed to follow, their true purposes were, and remain, an example to Christians generally.

The Origins of the Malta Degree

The source of the degree of Knight Templar has been discussed in chapter 3 and we had the temerity to propose the Rite of Strict Observance as a 'probable'. Whether or not it was purely the invention of von Hund or whether he was inspired by a forerunner it is impossible to say. We cannot, alas, look to that rite as the cradle of the Malta degree nor can we be so rash as to point, with assumed conviction, to some other masonic setting for its origin. The early reference in Ireland, in Dean Swift's parody of 1724 (*see* chapter 3), is interesting but is no indication of a masonic degree. It has reluctantly to be admitted that it has so far been impossible to discover a date and a location for the origin of the masonic Order of Malta.

It cannot be doubted that, whoever drew up the first ritual, it was strongly influenced by what was known of the medieval Order and its subsequent history. We have already seen that the officers of a masonic Priory of Malta derive their titles from those of the Hospitallers and its furnishings must surely reflect non-masonic practice of an earlier age.

When the evidence does begin, it shows that both the Templar and the Malta degrees were being worked in the same lodges, Royal Arch chapters and encampments before Dunckerley took command. It can be inferred from Baldwyn practice and from other records that in the very early days the two knighthoods would have been comprehended in one ceremony.

Curiously enough, two hundred years ago, the Grand Conclave was recorded as being that of '. . . Masonic Knights Templars . . . of St. John of Jerusalem, Palestine, Rhodes, &c'. It is, of course, perfectly logical to suppose that '*etcetera*' is here to be interpreted as 'Malta' (indeed, Baldwyn included that word in *their* title) but it was not until the 1850s that an insert in the *Statutes* as published in 1853 adds 'Malta, & the Mediterranean Pass'. By this time it can be seen that two separate degrees were regularly being conferred, that of Malta usually coming second although instances are known of the sequence being reversed.

It was the Templar ritual which first engaged the attention of Grand Conclave and an official version was promulgated in 1851 and proved generally acceptable. There followed in 1866 one for Malta and this too was readily adopted. Rituals are discussed in some detail in chapter 13, and the introduction of separate clothing and insignia for Knights of Malta receives mention in chapter 14.

13
RITUAL

Early Manuscript Books

IN THE ARCHIVES of Great Priory are many hand-written books of ritual which enable us to note developments and changes and to see how the traditional workings of such encampments as Baldwyn vary from those which are familiar to us today. Not all can be precisely dated and there are later copies of what are said to be earlier manuscripts.

One especially interesting copy made in 1877 is given as being of a ritual of about 1780 which includes catechetical lectures. Another dates from 1830, when Alexander Dalziel wrote out an extensive revision of the workings used in Royal Kent Encampment, Newcastle-on-Tyne, covering 'Knights of the Temple, Red Cross and Sepulchre of Jerusalem, Knights of Rhodes and Palestine, Knights of Malta, Mediterranean Pass, Pelican and Eagle, Harodim, Kadosh'; although not comprehended in the title, it also includes a short ceremony for Ne Plus Ultra. G. E. W. Bridge made a transcript of this 'Dalziel' ritual in which he comments that, 'subject to this "revision", it may be taken as one of the forms of the Knight Templar group current at the beginning of the nineteenth century, and may even be that worked by the lodges on the north-east coast in the eighteenth century'.

Standard Rituals

With Grand Conclave's promulgation on 10 April 1851, after due consideration, of an official ritual for the Knight Templar degree we come closer to the ceremonial which we practise today. At this stage we are still talking about note-books in which it had all been laboriously copied out by hand. For some time to come (certainly up to 1871, for which there is an example in the archives) it would have been the duty of an accomplished calligrapher in the 'Chancellerie' of the Orders – then at 14 Bedford Row, London WC – to prepare copies for transmission to Provincial Commanders who would make arrangements for dissemination to the encampments. In the process, of course, variations would arise and local customs would perhaps be allowed to survive in some details. Interesting specimens which have been returned to Great Priory include those which were the property of some of the most senior members of the Orders, including for instance Shadwell Clerke, and there are in them sundry annotations which deserve close attention in some future study.

These observations apply equally to the Malta ritual which was 'approved by the Committee' on 1 December 1866. There are books which contain both ceremonies, and one which includes also the Baldwyn working and some catechetical lectures. One of the great treasures in the archives is a volume superbly bound in red leather, with gilt embellishments. The 1851/1866 rituals, together with a consecration ceremony, written therein are masterpieces of the calligrapher's art and there are delightful illuminations which enhance its value.

Masson's System of Examination

John Masson, who was at the time Grand Chancellor in Grand Conclave, may justly be compared with William Preston, for what Preston had done for the Craft Masson endeavoured to do for the masonic Order of the Temple. Preston's work survives in the Emulation and other catechetic lectures which are still, if rather too rarely, delivered in lodges. Masson's perhaps deserved a better fate but it is to be feared that few knights of today would be willing to learn the questions and answers and thereby enlighten the minds of their brethren.

Nevertheless, in 1858 Grand Conclave thought so highly of it that its promulgation was approved. It was first published, in printed form, in three booklets in marbled card covers.

The first – after a dedication (signed by hand in each copy) to the Grand Master, Kemeys Tynte – contained the questions; the second had the answers, and in the third was a lecture 'embodying the origin of the Order; the rise and progress; the suppression; the masonic revival; the benefits resulting and the hoped for reward'. The revival here referred to, with scant justification, was based on a continuous thread passing through Scotland.

The Convent General's Ritual

In chapter 9 was mentioned the commission appointed by the Convent General to create a ritual and the ill favour with which their product was received. As we are about to learn, printed ceremonials were being introduced; these were in forms previously approved by Grand Conclave and, in the circumstances, were made especially welcome.

The Rituals of 'A Lewis'

'A Lewis' (not 'A. Lewis', as so often misprinted) was the firm, owned by John Hogg, which from 1870 onwards produced rituals for the Craft and other degrees. (The present-day successors are known as 'Lewis Masonic', the publishers of this book.) By 1876 they had issued *The Perfect Ceremonies of the Royal, Exalted, Religious and Military Order of Masonic Knights Templar*, which included the Malta and Mediterranean Pass workings and also Masson's System of Examination. It was, they said with justification, a copy of the ritual agreed to at the Grand Conclave for England and Wales and, because of its ready acceptance, there were several reprints. In none, however, was there any reference to the Convent General; Grand Conclave continued to be mentioned as the source, certainly up to the 1891 edition by when the title was referring to 'the United Orders'. It has been mentioned in an earlier chapter that 'A Lewis' was also producing in one volume the rituals just described together with that of the 'Rose Croix de Heredom', the latter being 'a copy of the ritual of the Supreme Council of the 33° for England and Wales' and here again its similarity to earlier manuscript workings and to the much more recent officially printed versions shows that it could be, and was, taken as authentic. Combined editions were brought out to about the turn of the century, by which time of course Great Priory was in full swing.

Great Priory Rituals

In 1900 came the first of Great Priory's own official rituals and these have since been amended, revised and reprinted on numerous occasions; their use has from the first been obligatory except for a few 'time immemorial' bodies. Among the revisions was one in 1900 which replaced the longer opening and closing exchanges (of 1851) between the Preceptor and the Constables with the present version, although preceptories which had been in existence before that year have always been permitted to retain the older one.

Until the 1970s, the official issues (with very rare exceptions) have included both Templar and Malta workings, but the two are now published separately with extended rubrics.

Here and there an individualist has compiled and printed a version exclusively for his own preceptory: for Grosvenor No. 132 at Chester George Harrison, still in 1920 calling himself the Eminent Commander, produced one bound in red leather which included the old opening and closing for the Templar degree but otherwise generally conformed. The copy in the archives is endorsed to the effect that, despite its unauthorized first issue (in 1920), Great Priory allowed its use until its author's death in 1930 – a kindly touch. In other instances – St. Salem at Macclesfield is one – locally printed inserts for the 1851 work are used.

Reference has been made elsewhere to the ritual for Baldwyn and other encampments/conclaves/preceptories which enjoy 'time immemorial' rights in their workings, some of which combine the Malta and Templar degrees in the one ceremony. Antiquity at Bath is probably unique in that it has its own printed formulary for the opening and closing, which is like that at Baldwyn, but prescribes that the official ritual shall otherwise be followed save for the interesting feature, after the investiture of the new knight, when a 'cook' enters with his large knife and warns that any departure from the vows now taken will require him to hack off the spurs of the offender! This feature can also be witnessed at Bristol.

William Tucker's 'Service' of 1850

Another treasure in the archives requires the introduction of William Tucker (1815-55), whose full story was admirably told in *AQC* 83 (1970) by John Cooper. At the age of only 31 he became Provincial Grand Master for Dorset and was admitted to the new Supreme Council for the Ancient and Accepted Rite, in which he later served briefly as Grand Secretary General. He is perhaps best remembered for what might be termed his masonic eccentricity, for he appeared in his Provincial Grand Lodge in 1853, not only in his Craft regalia but wearing over it the robe that in those days distinguished Sovereign Grand Inspectors General 33°. He there gave an address, highly injudicious for the ruler of a Craft Province, in which he claimed that Christianity was the basis of Freemasonry. For the two offences he was removed from his Craft appointment.

Let us now turn to his membership of our Orders. Kemeys Tynte's register does not say where or when Tucker was installed as a knight[1] but we read that he had joined Union or Rougemont at Exeter in 1843. Then in 1844 he was, with his friend Tynte, a founder of Holy Cross 'Conclave' which was to meet at Coryton Park, near Axminster, Tucker's seat. He was its Commander in 1846 and was in the same year appointed First Grand Standard Bearer by Tynte, the new Grand Master; in the following year he became Provincial Grand Commander for Dorset.

And in 1848 we find him as Commander of All Souls' Encampment at Weymouth. With all his other masonic activities we can see that William Tucker was whole-heartedly attached to Freemasonry.

The treasure already mentioned was a remarkable product of Tucker's fertile mind: *Officium Militum Templi. The Service of the Knights of the Temple and St. John of Jerusalem of the Holy Cross Conclave.* A red cloth-bound volume, printed in black and red, it is a collection of prayers, lessons, psalms, etc. These were intended to be added, at specified points, to the ceremonials for the Templar, Malta, Rose Croix and Ne Plus Ultra degrees and would have added enormously to the length of the proceedings. The Athanasian, Nicene and Apostles' Creeds are included, as is the Te Deum, and there is a strong hint of the Anglican service of Holy Communion in such terms as 'Collect, Epistle and Gospel' and by the inclusion — for the Ne Plus Ultra — the verses from 1 Corinthians 11 which an ordained priest alone may use at the Eucharist.

Almost all of the text is in both Latin and English. Although a number of divines were members, it must be doubted whether the others could have taken part in the Latin version. Nevertheless this publication must have had the blessing of the Grand Master, Kemeys Tynte, and a second edition, in stiff card covers, was printed in the same year.

In 1852 a warrant was granted for a separate Rose Croix chapter (now Coryton and Rougemont, at Exeter) and, as we have learned, a new and official ritual had been brought out in 1851, so Tucker's remarkable 'Service' must quite rapidly have fallen into desuetude. The Holy Cross Conclave moved to Plymouth and by 1893 had ceased to meet.

Ireland and Scotland

We have neither the space nor the materials to enable us to consider the development of the rituals in our sister Constitutions. Interest is, however, often expressed in the variations which can be witnessed when visiting beyond our own borders and, so far as we can with propriety set them down, a few observations are made on the workings currently in use.

In the Irish Craft and other degrees, the use of printed rituals is officially frowned upon, except perhaps overseas. There are in Dublin Grand Lodges and Grand Chapters of Instruction at which brethren attend to learn their duties as officers in their respective bodies. There is indeed a Great Preceptory of Instruction for the United Orders which meets four times a year for a like purpose, but the Great Priory also issues printed ceremonials from which the wording and many of the rubrics can be learned at home.

Scotland similarly furnishes official rituals which are well rubricated and a supplementary *Guide to Ceremonial* which, as well as teaching its own knights how to carry out their work, enable a qualified student to examine and compare his own practices with those of his brethren north of the border.

Let it be said at once that the ceremonies of the three Constitutions have a very great deal in common and that visitors in either direction would have no difficulty at all in feeling very much at home. The arrangement of a Chapel of the Order of the Temple is at first sight similar in all three, but that which, in England, we are accustomed to seeing in the centre of the apartment is absent in Ireland and Scotland, where the standards are placed in the east rather than in the west.

Brief mention is made in chapter 15 of the titles of certain officers of a Scottish preceptory and their places in the chapel are, in several instances, quite different from those occupied by the equivalent ranks in England.

There are variations in the sequence of events and in the texts which are followed but these, and many other most interesting features, may not here be pursued. What is important is that, in each of our three Constitutions, the candidate learns the same lessons and is inspired by the same high ideals which have characterized the masonic Order of the Temple from its earliest days.

Precisely the same can be said of the Order of Malta, in which however the similarities outweigh the differences.

[1] It is elsewhere recorded that he was installed on 16 June 1843 in the Cross of Christ Encampment, London. He joined the Exeter Encampment on 19 October.

14

CLOTHING AND JEWELS

UNLIKE THE ENGLISH Craft, for which the prescribed dress has always been an apron, with perhaps a collar and jewel as a brother takes office, the masonic Knight Templar has been subject to quite radical changes in what he is expected to wear.

In Dunckerley's Day

The *Statutes* of 1791 referred to an obligatory sash and medal, but we learn from one of his letters at the end of that year that he was supplying 'sashes, stars and crosses' to an encampment, the cost of three of each being a modest £3.6s.0d! Only a month later he was giving much more detail:

> I have sent a Uniform button and pattern of the Cloth for a Frock to be worn, which I have established to be worn in the several Conclaves. The Coat will take 14 Buttons, ten in front & four for the hips, & shirts with two very small gilt buttons at the opening of each sleeve, and a White Kersymer Waistcoat & White French casket buttons, with black breeches. A cheap suit of Clothes that may be worn by men of all professions, and at any time. I paid the Taylor £4.4s.0d. for my Coat & Waistcoat. In all the Chapters Cock'd Hats and Cockades are worn with Swords and black velvet stocks. The Stocks, Cockades & Swords to be kept in a box at each Chapter.
> Most of the Knights (I have more than 120 registered) have already appeared in their uniforms . . .

It may be recalled that the Grand Scribe's letter of 14 February 1805 (reproduced in chapter 4) set out the Duke of Kent's 'request' as to jewels and regalia, repeated here for ready reference:

> The Grand Commander a Star of eight points with a black Sash over the right shoulder; the Captains a similar Sash with a Star of seven points; Private Companions the same Sash with a Mother of Pearl Cross, and all

> to wear an Apron bound with black with the proper Skull and Cross-Bones displayed thereon; and for the sake of uniformity we think that a Suit of Black and black Sword would be more consistent with the Order than any other dress.

It is curious that these quite detailed provisions were not repeated in the second issue of *Statutes* of 1809. (These, incidentally, were the subject of A.C.F. Jackson's 'Early Statutes of the Knights Templar' in *AQC* 89 (1976) and are set out in full therein.)

From a short history (*circa* 1917) of the Antient York Conclave of Redemption we learn that the sash was of black watered silk, four inches broad with fringed ends, the cross was of silver and the star was seven-pointed, with a motto. A black cap and a black sword were also being worn in the Conclave 'under the 1791 *Statutes*', which do not in fact mention headwear and weapons!

In the Nineteenth Century

After the 1809 edition, the next issue of *Statutes* was not until 1846, when Kemeys Tynte became Grand Master, and the relevant rule has been rather enigmatically amended to read 'in the proper costume of the Order'. In 1853, however, came an entirely rewritten set of *Statutes*, very obviously inspired by the contemporary Craft *Constitutions*, and here, under 'As to Costume', are for the first time, several pages of most detailed instructions on the Badge [apron], Sash or Baldric, Sword, Crosses, Star, Cloak or Mantle, Gauntlets, and Collars and Jewels to be worn by Officers and Past Officers. There are several illustrations of the various forms of Cross and of jewels of office.

The sashes, both plain and differentiated, were precisely the same as those which the most recent revision of our rules lays down. The collars, from which jewels of office were suspended, matched the sashes. In other items of regalia there would be many more alterations to come.

We are fortunate in that our archives have two photographs (plates 13 and 19), one early and one more recent, to illustrate this regalia. The engraving of the Oxford Ball (plate 12) may also be of interest in this respect. In several masonic halls, Knight Templar aprons are among the exhibits behind glass and many varieties of embellishment can be seen.

Convent General

It has been mentioned in chapter 9 that in 1873 there were proposals in Convent General for quite radical changes in dress. The apron disappeared, except for those who had already entered the Order. A tunic was provided for as were the variations in the mantle which still distinguish those who have been installed as Preceptors. A completely different habit for Knights of Malta was added to the regulations and this too has scarcely changed. It would seem that caps and their badges were also among the innovations.

Towards the end of the rule of the Convent General, among measures which were intended to stave off disaster was the restoration of the mantle-badge. When it had been first introduced is not known, but it must have been after 1853 because at that time badges of rank were of metal and were worn at the point of the collar. A centenary jewel was first authorized in 1888 for Jerusalem Preceptory No. 5.

Knights Grand Cross and Knights Commander

In 1900 it was enjoined that holders of these high honours should henceforth enjoy concurrent designations in both Orders, namely G.C.T./G.C.M. and K.C.T./K.C.M., and distinctive sashes were prescribed.

Ireland and Scotland

The present-day dress for our sister Constitutions is broadly similar to our own, in that tunics, mantles, caps, gauntlets, belts and swords are *de rigueur*. There are, however many differences in detail and especially so in Scotland where variations in headdress according to rank are perhaps the most immediately noticed. Perhaps the most interesting addition, 'desirable' for a Scottish knight, is that of buff leather boots, reaching above the knee, with gilt spurs and red leathers.

Plate 1
Left and below:
THE CHURCH OF THE HOLY SEPULCHRE, CAMBRIDGE

(Photograph by courtesy of Woodmansterne)

Plate 2
LAMBERT DE LINTOT'S DESIGN OF 1785 FOR HIS RITE OF SEVEN DEGREES

Plate 3
AS USED BY DUNCKERLEY ON EARLY HAND-WRITTEN GRAND CONCLAVE CERTIFICATES
with some of the previous wording obliterated.

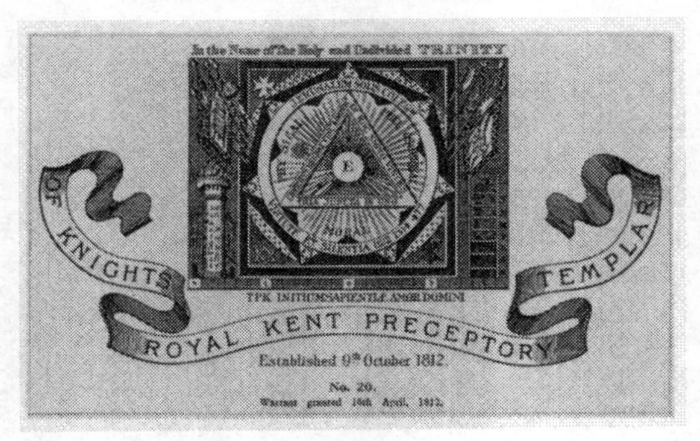

Plate 4
ROYAL KENT PRECEPTORY, NEWCASTLE-UPON-TYNE
The summonses of this preceptory perpetuate the use of the De Lintot design, as modified by Dunckerley

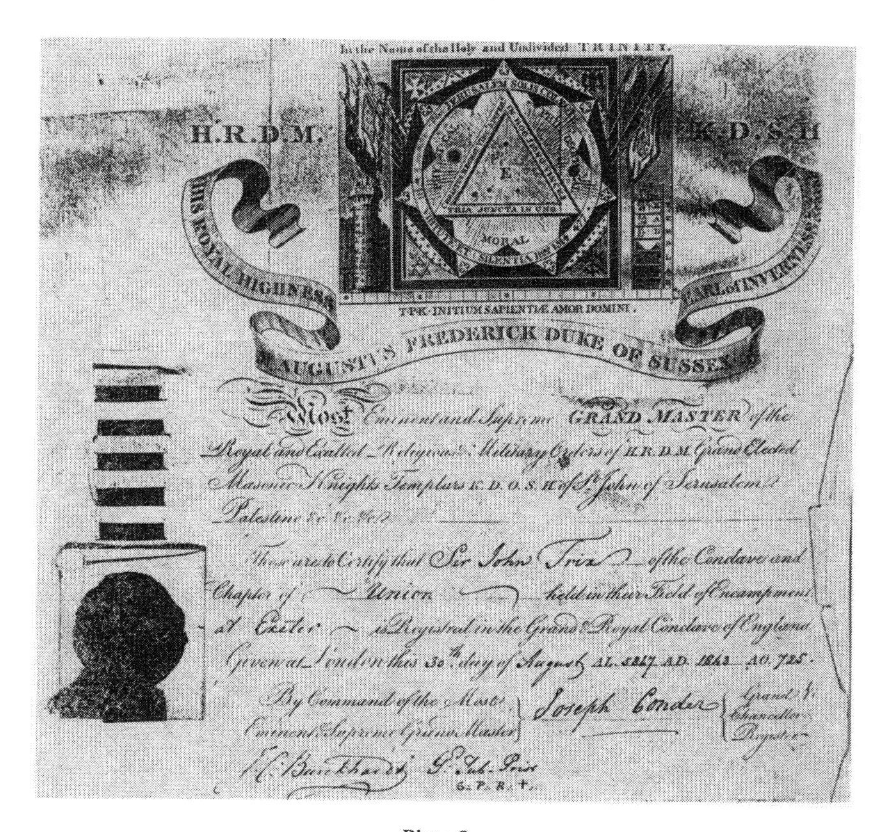

In the Name of the Holy and Undivided TRINITY.

H.R.D.M. K.D.S.H

HIS ROYAL HIGHNESS AUGUSTUS FREDERICK DUKE OF SUSSEX EARL of INVERNESS

T.P.K. INITIUM SAPIENTIÆ AMOR DOMINI.

Most Eminent and Supreme GRAND MASTER of the Royal and Exalted Religious & Military Orders of H.R.D.M. Grand Elected Masonic Knights Templars K.D.S.H. of St. John of Jerusalem Palestine &c. &c. &c.

These are to Certify that Sir John Trix of the Conclave and Chapter of Union held in their Field of Encampment at Exeter is Registred in the Grand & Royal Conclave of England Given at London this 30th day of August AL. 5847 AD. 1843 AO. 725.

By Command of the Most Eminent & Supreme Grand Master Joseph Conder Grand Chancellor Register

Burckhardt Gd. Sub-Prior G.P.R.+

Plate 5

A PRINTED GRAND CONCLAVE CERTIFICATE OF 1843

There had been more than one re-engraving of the design by this time. This certificate, issued to John Trix of the Conclave and Chapter of Union at Exeter, is of particular interest because the Duke of Sussex had died some months before. Burckhardt, by way of authentication, has countersigned as Grand Sub-Prior and Sovereign Prince Rose Croix.

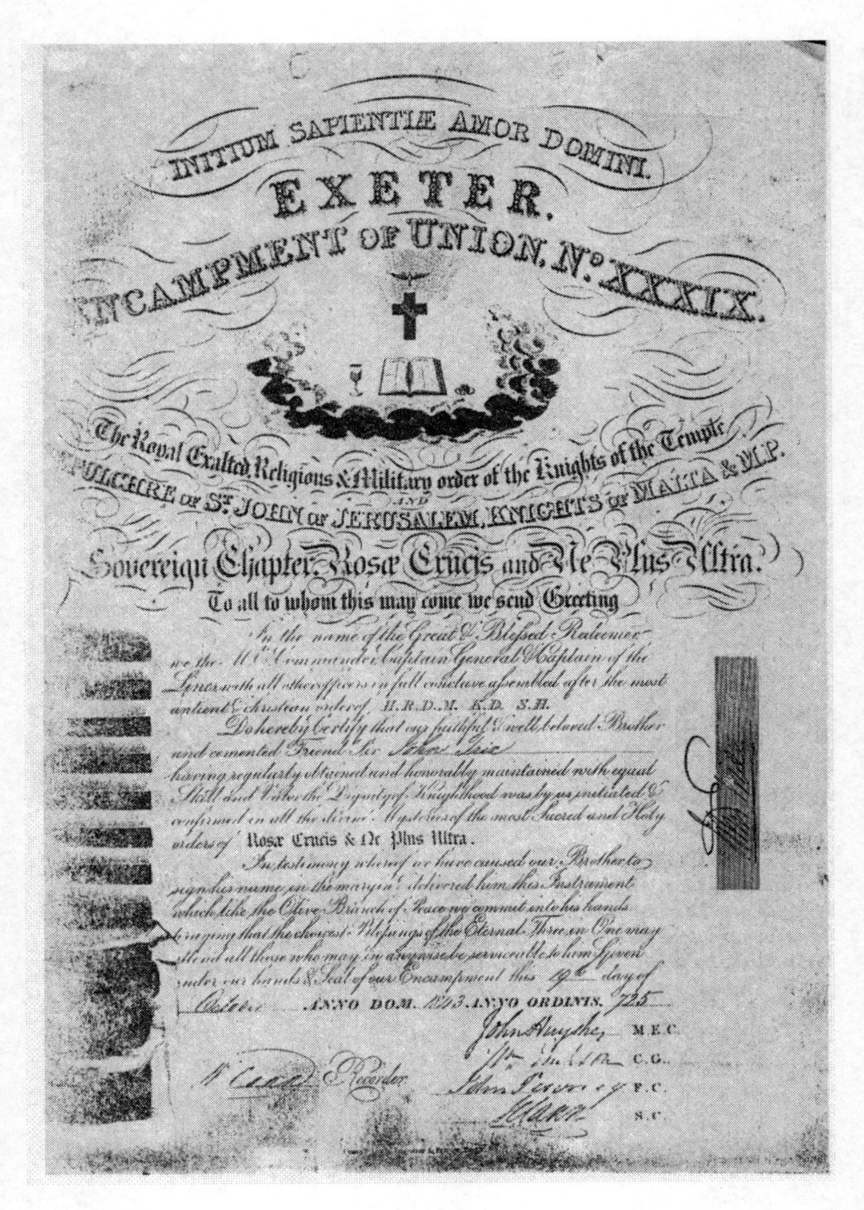

INITIUM SAPIENTIÆ AMOR DOMINI.

EXETER.

ENCAMPMENT OF UNION, No. XXXIX.

The Royal Exalted Religious & Military order of the Knights of the Temple and Sepulchre of St. John of Jerusalem, Knights of Malta & M.P.

Sovereign Chapter, Rosæ Crucis and Ne Plus Ultra.

To all to whom this may come we send Greeting

In the name of the Great & Blessed Redeemer we the M.E. Commander Captain General & Captain of the Lines with all other officers in full conclave assembled after the most antient & christian order of H.R.D.M. K.D. S.H.

Do hereby Certify that our faithful & well beloved Brother and cemented Friend Sir John Trix having regularly obtained and honorably maintained with equal Skill and Valor the Dignity of Knighthood was by us initiated & confirmed in all the divine Mysteries of the most Sacred and Holy orders of Rosæ Crucis & Ne Plus Ultra.

In testimony whereof we have caused our Brother to sign his name in the margin & delivered him this Instrument which like the Olive Branch of Peace we commit into his hands hoping that the choicest Blessings of the Eternal Three in One may attend all those who may in anywise be serviceable to him. Given under our hands & Seal of our Encampment this [illegible] day of October ANNO DOM. 1843 ANNO ORDINIS. 725

John Huyshe M.E.C.

[illegible] C.G.

[illegible] Recorder

John [illegible] F.C.

[illegible] S.C.

Plate 6

ENCAMPMENT OF UNION, EXETER

This is typical of locally issued certificates of the period. It records that John Trix (see also plate 5) has been advanced to the Rose Croix and Ne Plus Ultra degrees. There is an added interest in that the Commander of the encampment, who has signed the document, was the Reverend John Huyshe, who later became Deputy Grand Master (1861-72).

Plate 7
THOMAS DUNCKERLEY
Grand Master, 1791-1795
Portrait in oils by Thomas Beach, owned by Loyal Lodge No.251, Barnstaple.

Plate 8
HRH EDWARD, DUKE OF KENT AND STRATHEARN
Royal Grand Patron, 1791-1805, 1807-1820
Grand Master, 1805-1807
Engraving by Roberts, published 1820.

Plate 9
HRH AUGUSTUS FREDERICK, DUKE OF SUSSEX,
Earl of Inverness, Baron Arklow
Grand Master, 1812-1843
Unattributed portrait, c.*1820, owned by the Masonic Trust for Girls and Boys.*

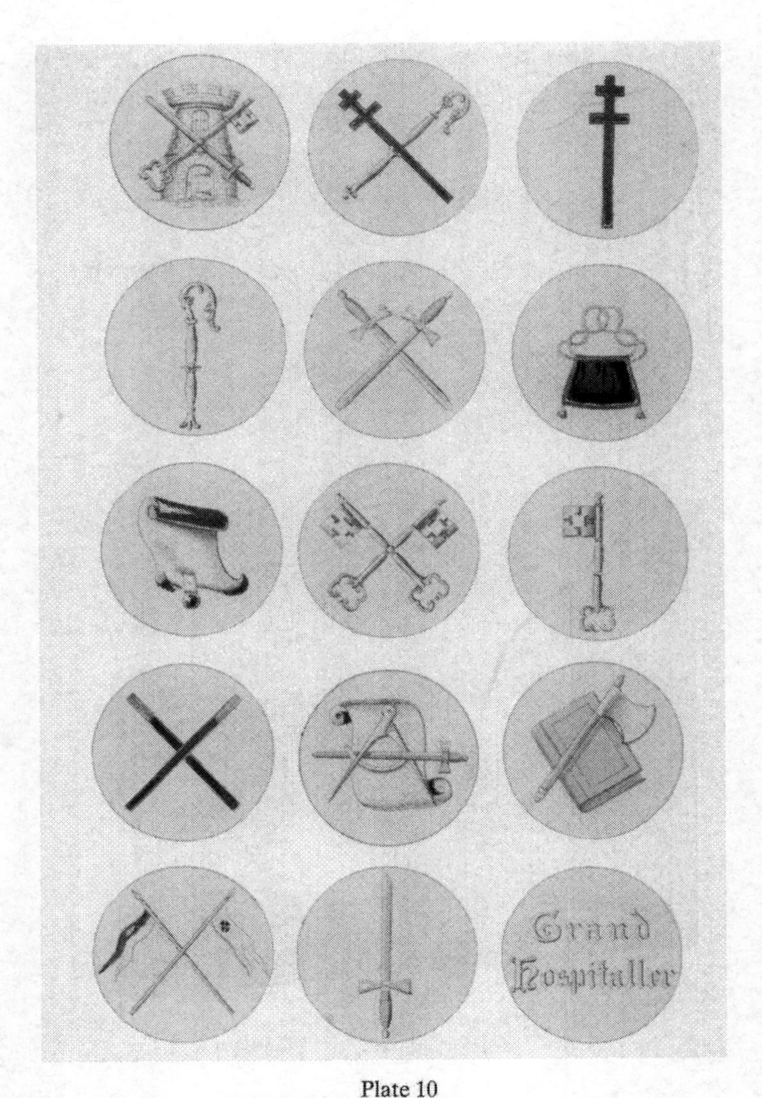

Plate 10

BADGES OF OFFICE IN GRAND CONCLAVE, 1853-1872

These designs, taken from the 1864 Statutes, *were for the devices which appeared in the centres of the collar jewels. The jewels were in the form of a red Cross Patêe, three inches across, with a circular centre of one-and-a-quarter inches. The devices here shown are, respectively, for the Grand Seneschal, Prior, Sub-Prior, Prelate, Captains, Chancellor and Vice-Chancellor, Registrar, Chamberlain, Director of Ceremonies, Constable, Provost, Banner Bearer, and Sword Bearer. The devices for the Grand Hospitaller, Almoner, Experts, Standard Bearer, Warden of the Regalia, Aides-de-Camp, Captains of Lines, Heralds, Organist and Equerry bore only the name of the office. The collars were four inches wide, of black watered silk with the three white stripes which are preserved in the Great Officer's sash of today.*

Plate 11
WILLIAM STUART
Grand Master, 1861-1872
Portrait in oils at Mark Masons' Hall

Plate 12

THE OXFORD MASONIC BALL, 1863

On 16 June 1863, Apollo University Lodge No.357 gave a Ball in the New Corn Exchange, Oxford, for the Prince and Princess of Wales, who had been married in March of that year. Her Royal Highness danced only a few sets of quadrilles and lancers, but — so the report has it — the Prince 'was indefatigable, and stood up in every set till supper time, at twelve o'clock. The engraving is of great interest masonically because it portrays the reception of the royal guests under an arch of steel

which must have been formed by knights from the Coeur de Lion Encampment, wearing — as was at the time appropriate — their aprons and mantles. Both collars and sashes are suggested by the artist but there is insufficient detail. The regalia worn by the brother second from the left is not easily recognizable and may owe much to the imagination of the artist. It gives a Templar rather than a Craft impression and its wearer may have been merely the Commander of the Bodyguard! It is a matter of some surprise that no Craft Freemasons are depicted in what was a Lodge Ball.
(Illustrated London News, 27 June 1863)

Plate 13

AN UNKNOWN KNIGHT, c.*1875*

The style and quality of this photograph place it in the 1870s, shortly after the establishment of the Convent General, when the apron became obsolete except for those in possession. As is typical of many masonic portraits of the time, the subject is very probably wearing the jewels of every Order to which he belonged. The Royal Arch and Mark are obvious; among the miniatures are those of the Temple and Malta, the Rose Croix and the Royal and Select Masters (whose Grand Council was formed in 1871). The neck jewel suggests that a high rank had been attained in the Ancient and Accepted Rite; the apron is that of a more junior knight. It will be observed that separate gauntlets are worn. The cut of the mantle, here somewhat casually draped, is more akin to that which is currently assumed in Scotland.

(Great Priory Archives)

Plate 14

HRH ALBERT EDWARD, PRINCE OF WALES

Grand Master of the Convent General, 1872-1895

There is no portrait in the archives which depicts the Prince as a Knight Templar. This relatively little-known picture, however, has the advantage of dating from the early part of his Templar Grand Mastership. In his regalia as ruler of the English Craft, the Prince stands in front of the throne on which so many Grand Masters have taken their seat.

(Drawn, lithographed and published by Bro Edward J. Harty, 1875)

Plate 15

COLONEL SHADWELL H. CLERKE

Great Sub-Prior, Convent General, 1873-1891

One does not often see a likeness of Brother Clerke and yet his name is familiar in masonic history and is borne by several masonic bodies. He was the Grand Secretary of the Craft from 1880 to 1891 and had previously served as the Grand Secretary General in the Ancient and Accepted Rite, in whose Supreme Council he continued in another office until his death. He wears the insignia of the 33° in this photograph. It will have been noted from chapter 9 that Brother Clerke was not a whole-hearted admirer of all that the Convent General tried to do.

Plate 16
EDWARD, 1st EARL OF LATHOM
Great Prior of England, Convent General, 1877-1896.
(Grand Lodge Library)

Plate 17

CHARLES FITZGERALD MATIER

Great Vice-Chancellor, 1896-1914

He is remembered with gratitude by all the Orders which, for so many years, he successfully administered. Born in 1840 or 1841, his masonic career began in Edinburgh where in 1869 he entered the Order of the Temple. He was by this time living in the Manchester area and, as a Scottish Royal Arch Mason, establishing Scottish Mark Masonry there, but that is another story. He was invested in 1873 as a Scottish Knight Commander of the Temple and he wears in this portrait the beaded collar of that dignity. The badge which he carries on his English-pattern mantle is that of a Scottish Grand Bearer of Vexillum Belli, but his sash is that of an English Great Officer. He joined the Preceptory of St George No.6 in London in 1886, and his neck jewel commemorates his Preceptorship in 1891. As he served for one year as Great Marshal in 1893, we are able to date this photograph very precisely in 1892. Brother Knight Matier was made a Knight Commander of England on St. Andrew's Day 1893 and was advanced to Knight Grand Cross on St George's Day 1902.

Plate 18
HENRY JAMES FITZROY, EARL OF EUSTON
Grand Master, 1896-1907; Pro Grand Master 1908-1912
Lord Euston's mantle, tunic and cap, and his other regalia make interesting comparison with those in portraits of later Grand Masters. His Cross of Salem, the jewel of his office, is here worn as a neck jewel. In addition to his insignia as a Knight Grand Cross in the United Orders he appears also to be wearing that of a Knight Grand Cross of the Order of the Red Cross of Constantine, of which he was at the time Grand Sovereign. Perhaps most noticeably, his sash is worn over the left shoulder.
(Great Priory Archives)

Plate 21
HENRY, 6th EARL OF HAREWOOD
Pro Grand Master, 1932-1939; Grand Master, 1939-1947
Unlike the Earl of Euston, Lord Harewood is wearing the steel chain which now forms part of the Grand Master's insignia and from which is suspended the Cross of Salem. Although in 1900 sashes or ribands of special design had been introduced for Knights Grand Cross and Knights Commander, Grand Masters seem to have preferred to wear that of a Great Officer, possibly by analogy with such Orders as the Garter and the Thistle in which the riband is worn only when the collar is not prescribed.
(Great Priory Archives)

Plate 22

GEORGE ST. VINCENT, 5th LORD HARRIS

Grand Master, 1947-1973

This photograph is a pleasant reminder of the visit of Great Priory to York in 1957. Followed by his Banner, the Grand Master advances beneath an arch of steel.

(Great Priory Archives)

Plate 23
THREE KNIGHTS IN 1961
Very Eminent Knight Lt.-Col. J. W. Chitty, M.B.E., G.C.T., Great Vice-Chancellor, Very Eminent Knight C. M. Jennings, K.C.T., Provincial Prior for Ceylon, and Very Eminent Knight Sir George Boag, K.C.S.I., C.I.E., K.C.T., Provincial Prior for Surrey, in a photograph taken on 6 February 1961. Sir George Boag had already had a distinguished masonic career in Madras, where he had ruled the Craft, Royal Arch and Mark from 1934 to 1946, but had assumed many new honours on his return to England. He died in 1969. Colonel Chitty, although he retired from his office in Great Priory in 1968, continues to serve Freemasonry as Supreme Ruler of the Order of the Secret Monitor. (In all three instances, the correct prefix would today be 'Right Eminent'.)
(Great Priory Archives)

Plate 24

TRI-PARTITE CONFERENCE AT DUBLIN, 1968

Taken in the splendid Knight Templars' Chapel in Freemasons' Hall, Dublin. Colonel Sir Basil McFarland, Grand Master of Ireland (1959-78) is flanked by Lord Harris of England and Sir Malcolm Barclay-Harvey of Kinord, Grand Master of Scotland (1967-9). The similarities and differences between the clothing of the three Constitutions can be clearly seen.

(Great Priory Archives)

Plate 25
T.H. BOYNE, UNITED STATES OF AMERICA
Sir Knight Boyne joined a preceptory under the Great Priory of England in 1930 and presented this imposing portrait of himself in the dress then, and in general still, worn by American knights. There are variations in detail; for instance in Arkansas black plumes adorn the chapeau *and it seems to be usual nowadays for shoulder badges to be worn.*
*(*Great Priory Archives*)*

15

OFFICERS

REFERENCE HAS ELSEWHERE been made to many of the changes in the titles of various offices held in the Order of the Temple, and in particular those brought about when the Convent General came into being. The roll of Grand Masters and Great Priors at Appendix G betrays, for instance, the fact that the position at one time held by a Deputy Grand Master is now occupied by the Great Seneschal.

The Earliest Years of Grand Conclave

The 1791 *Statutes* (reproduced at Appendix B) tell us of an 'acting Grand Master', Provincial Acting Grand Masters (at a distance from the metropolis), a Grand Chancellor, a Treasurer and a Grand Scribe and Register [*sic*]. We learn too that a 'complete chapter of the order is to consist of an eminent deputy grand master, two captains commanding columns, two standard-bearers with knights attendants, and one or two equeries [*sic*]'. The first three are to represent their encampments in Grand Conclave.

In the 1809 *Statutes* a Deputy Grand Master first comes to notice, as do First and Second Grand Captains, a Grand Prelate, and a Grand Register (also styled Grand Vice-Chancellor and Register), '. . . and all other acting Grand Officers of the said Order'. The Minutes of Grand Conclave in 1806 enlighten us as to some of these others and from sundry later Minutes we can find more to add to our list: A. G. Commander (presumably 'Acting Grand', in the absence of the Grand Master himself), Grand Sword Bearer, Master of *the* Ceremonies, Grand Chamberlain and Vice-Chamberlain, Grand Almoner, First and Second Grand Experts, Aids [*sic*] de (or 'du') Camp, Grand Herald, Captains of the Lines, Grand Orator and Keeper of the Archives, Grand Provosts and Hospitallers, Members of the Grand Council, Grand Equerry. There are too some rather exotic introductions, such as Grand Procurators General for Scotland (1810) and Hayti (1811) and a Superintendant [*sic*] for the Principality of Wales. True, there was an encampment on the island of Haiti in 1811, but one wonders what Grand Conclave had in mind for Scotland!

In 1811 two Captains General were added *below* the two Grand Captains and their number was increased to five in the following year. The Grand Register briefly became 'Registrar' in 1807 only but then reverted to the odd but time-honoured former designation which was used until the duties of Vice-Chancellor and Registrar were separated.

From 1846

The first official appearance of these divided functions was in the *Statutes* of 1846 when in a single list were added to most of the offices already encountered a Grand Prior, a Grand Sub-Prior, Provincial Grand Commanders, a Grand Organist, a Grand Banner Bearer (in addition to two Standard Bearers).

While there is no mention, other than a clue in the title of the Order, of a Malta degree as a separate entity, the presence among the Grand Officers now being specified of a Prior, Sub-Prior and Hospitaller is suggestive. From an examination of the ritual promulgated in 1866, it can be seen that virtually no change in the nomenclature of the Malta officers has occurred from that day to this.

Under Convent General

As has been reported in a previous chapter, Convent General did not often meet in formal assembly. In any other convention of the knights, the place in a procession and the seating of the Great Officers (for such they now were) from the two National Great Priories, and the 'Arch' officers of Convent General itself, must have been a problem even to the Great Experts who, as the equivalents of Deacons in the Craft, would have had some responsibility for solving it.

The Templar ritual of 1851, as later put into print, continued in use by preceptories throughout the years of the Convent General but it is interesting to find that, by the 1884 edition, 'recent changes' in the designations of officers were being notified on an extra page at the beginning. From this we must take note of a few alterations which had clearly emanated from the Convent General:

Commander	to	Preceptor
First Captain	to	Constable
Second Captain	to	Marshal
Expert	to	Sub Marshal

Unchanged were the Registrar, the Captains of Lines, the Equerry Without, and the Treasurer. The Marshal as a Director of Ceremonies had not yet arrived on the scene, but was what we now recognize as the Second Constable.

From 1895

With the independence of Great Priory began the series of final changes which resulted in the tallies of officers, at all levels, which we have today. At about the turn of the century appears evidence that Great Officers of the Temple were being accorded ranks in the Great Priory of Malta and were taking part in the ceremonies performed therein.

Offices in Provincial Priories have generally corresponded with those at higher level. A very recent development has been the introduction of London and Overseas Rank, with their own distinctive mantle badges. The first knights to be so honoured were invested by the Great Seneschal, Lord Swansea, on 25 October 1989 in Connaught Army and Navy Preceptory No.172.

Ireland

Bearing in mind that the Irish Great Priory was, with that of England, governed from 1872 to 1895 by the Convent General, it is not surprising that – in both the Templar and Malta degrees – the Great Officers and the officers of a preceptory bear the same names and carry out the same duties as their counterparts under the Great Priory of England. Their places in a 'Chapel of the Order of the Temple' or in a 'Chapter House of the Order of Knights Hospitallers' differ in some respects from those with which we are familiar and, for the Templar degree, a Conductor plays some part in escorting the candidate. (The Conductor has a similar role in Irish Craft working.)

Scotland

Although the governing body for Scotland has long been known as the Great Priory, its officers are 'Grand' rather than 'Great' and the tallies at all levels include some titles unknown in England. In a preceptory are found a Sub-Preceptor (comparable with the Depute Master in a Scottish lodge), a Seneschal and only one Constable; the bearer of the Beauceant is the Beaucennifer and there is a Secretary to carry out the administrative duties. At the octagonal table in the Priory of Malta, Bearers of the Banners of St. John and Malta and a Herald sit in the places of our Admiral, Baillie and Turcopolier.

16

THE UNITED ORDERS ABROAD

WE HAVE so far confined ourselves to the beginnings and early development of the masonic Orders of the Temple and Malta in Great Britain and Ireland. As with other Orders and degrees, however, those with which we are concerned — in various forms and by varying paths — sooner or later reached many of those countries overseas into which the Craft had been introduced by brethren from the 'home' Grand Lodges.

THE UNITED STATES

St. Andrew's Royal Arch Lodge, Boston

The earliest Minute to tell us of the installation of a Knight Templar abroad (or indeed anywhere) is precisely dated — 28 August 1769 — and travelling British regimental lodges played no small part in the events of that day in Boston, Massachusetts. A brief reference was made in chapter 3, but so relevant to our story is it that the occasion earns rather more extended treatment here.

St. Andrew's Lodge No. 81 had been established at Boston under a Scottish charter very appropriately dated on St. Andrew's Day, 30 November 1756. There was, too, a St. Andrew's *Royal Arch* Lodge which, although its written records begin on 18 August 1769 — only ten days before the meeting we are soon to describe, must have met before then. In 1762 the Craft lodge had, without success, asked the Grand Lodge at Edinburgh (at that date there was no such thing as a Grand Chapter anywhere) for a warrant for the Royal Arch, reporting that 'a sufficient number of us have arrived at that sublime degree'. We cannot here fully debate on how and where they had done so; the Lodge at Fredericksburg in Virginia had made Royal Arch masons in 1753, but the regimental lodges did not arrive in America until October 1768. From then on these would have been prepared to dispense the ultra-Craft degrees which were, at the time and for many years after, being conferred on the somewhat tenuous authority of their Irish and Antient warrants.

Sir Charles Cameron (*AQC* 13, 1900, page 157) concluded, after studying the centenary records of St. Andrew's [Craft] Lodge, that the most likely source of the Templar working of that day in 1769 was the Irish lodge in the 29th Foot, that regiment being in Boston at the time.

Turnbull and Denslow, in *A History of Royal Arch Masonry* (1956), think it likely that these military lodges had sponsored and organized the Royal Arch Lodge at Boston. This, although the records of St. Andrew's [Craft] Lodge nowhere mention its existence, claimed to work under the authority of the latter. In 1790, by which time it was known as St. Andrew's Royal Arch *Chapter*, it passed a vote of thanks to the lodge for the use of their warrant which, incidentally, was not surrendered to Edinburgh until 1809, when the lodge adhered to the Grand Lodge of Massachusetts, which had already been in operation for seventeen years.

St. Andrew's Chapter, one of the seven in New England which established the General Grand Chapter of the United States in 1797, also played a part in founding the Grand Chapter of Massachusetts in 1798-9, then as now admitting the supreme authority of the General Grand Chapter.

The Boston Minute

We must, however, return to that meeting of 28 August 1769. In St. Andrew's Royal Arch Lodge, William Davis – a Past Master of Lodge No 58 (Antient) in the 14th Regiment of Foot (a lodge formed in 1759 but no longer working by the Union of 1813) – 'begging to have and receive the Parts belonging to a Royal Arch Mason . . . was accordingly made by receiving the four Steps, that of an Excellt., Sup., Royal Arch and Kt.Templar'. Also there were two other members of No 58, with three of Lodge 322 (Irish) in the 29th Foot (already mentioned), and three of the Royal Arch Lodge itself. It seems reasonable to suppose that all save the candidate had already taken the four steps in their own or other lodges or chapters and were therefore Knights Templar. To know *when* they had been so advanced would be a valuable addition to our chronology!

We know that Lodge No 322 had been warranted in 1759 while the regiment was serving in Ireland. Now known as 'Glittering Star', in the Worcestershire and Sherwood Foresters Regiment, it is one of the two surviving lodges, from a tally of more than 400, which are empowered by their warrants to travel.

The Halifax 'Inference'

It is interesting to find, in an excellent little history (1966) of Lodge Glittering Star by R. V. Harris (who was an eminent Canadian masonic writer), not only a detailed account of the period in Boston, but also what he classifies as an 'irresistible inference' that the lodge would have been conferring the Royal Arch and Templar degrees in Halifax, Nova Scotia, in 1765-8. The no less eminent Irish historian Philip Crossle, in writing to Harris, gave firm support to the inference as, he said, '[the degrees] are known to have been worked in Ireland from about 1740'.

The Grand Encampment of the United States

The degree of Knight Templar continued to be worked in St. Andrew's Chapter until 1794, by which time there had been numerous instances of its conferment elsewhere in the eastern states of America, and — as had happened in England — encampments of the Order were being formed. An early Grand Encampment of 1795 at Philadelphia did not last long but others followed and, by 1816, a *General* Grand Encampment was under way. This (it has dropped the first word of the title) remains the supreme authority in the United States, with forty-seven state Grand Commanderies under its control, as well as Grand Commanderies and individual commanderies which have been established in other countries by American knights temporarily or permanently living abroad.

Dress

It would take a very long chapter indeed to detail the many differences between British and American practice in the United Orders. In visual terms the most obvious must be that of dress for our brother knights in the United States wear a black military-style uniform with a cocked hat which they call 'the *chapeau*'. There have been proposals for abandoning this outfit, which is costly, in exchange for something more like our own. But the American knights have a great affection for their dress, so much so that instances are recorded of its being worn at weddings, with an arch of steel as the knightly groom and his bride leave the church!

Impressive indeed on the great public occasions are the marching commanderies, drilled to perfection. An excellent description of just such an occasion appears in our *Liber Ordinis Templi* for 1905, reporting on the visit of the then Grand Master, the Earl of Euston, with his Great Vice-Chancellor, C. F. Matier, and other Great Officers to the 29th Triennial Conclave of the Grand Encampment at San Francisco. One paragraph in particular catches the eye:

> The Parade and Escort [with the English visitors in open carriages with their hosts] started punctually at the appointed hour, and in the most brilliant sunshine, . . . marched by a winding route of four miles through the streets . . . There were over 11,000 Knights Templar in line, accompanied by sixty-three bands of music and several drum corps. Over 250,000 people viewed the procession, which was one of the most magnificent pageants ever seen in America, and took nearly three hours in passing the reviewing stand.

It is highly probable that, among the band music will have been marches composed by Sir Knight John Philip Sousa for he wrote several for masonic use, still in the repertoire today.

This colourful description, by substituting white open limousines for the carriages, would serve as well for the present-day Triennial Conclaves in America. It is a source of pleasure that the warm relationship which then existed between our American brother knights and ourselves is no less evident today.

Ritual

One of the strangest features to us of the American United Orders is that there are three rather than two: those of the Red Cross, Malta and the Temple, taken in that sequence. The first does not in itself involve the Christian faith. (In England we know it as one of the Allied Degrees; in Scotland it is worked as the Babylonish Pass in their Royal Arch system; in Ireland it is now under an independent Order of Knight Masons. There is also a relationship, which we will not here pursue, with certain degrees of the Ancient and Accepted Rite.)

The costume for the Malta degree is not unlike our own and the full ceremonial would also be familiar to us. There is, however, a shortened version which enables both the Malta and Templar degrees to be worked on the same evening and this seems to be the more frequent practice. Until 1916 the Templar working preceded that of Malta, both being performed in full.

While in earlier times the American ritual for the Order of the Temple was derived from the contemporary English version, it had by the middle of the nineteenth century added to it the strongly military characteristics which are so evident today.

DEVELOPMENTS ELSEWHERE

The Army Lodges

In reviewing the introduction of the masonic Templar and Malta Orders into other parts of the world, the role of the regimental lodges must again be borne in mind. The first such lodge was authorized in 1732 but it was to be quite a few years before we can be sure that any of them discovered the extra degrees which were, so to speak, coming into circulation. When they did so, many of them embraced with zeal and pleasure the opportunity of varying their routine (as did the stationary lodge in Ireland whose annual programme of many years later was mentioned in chapter 3). Ample authority for the practice of ultra-Craft degrees was, as we have seen, believed to be inherent in Irish and Antient warrants. George Draffen (*Pour la Foy*, 1949, page 13) affirms that it was the usual custom — and he is referring to the years 1778 to 1790 — for Scottish lodges to take a similar view. And many under the premier Grand Lodge followed suit.

The founding of the Grand Conclave in 1791 was not too speedily followed by the establishment of overseas encampments. It will have been observed that, among those which Dunckerley claimed to have taken under his wing was the Fortitude Encampment in the 1st Dragoon Guards. This had ceased to exist by 1809, as had a travelling Craft lodge in the regiment, warranted by the premier Grand Lodge in 1780. It was not until 1811 and 1812 that two encampments were formed in the West Indies, very probably short-lived. In 1824 came the first of several in Canada, and in 1840, at Calcutta, the first in India. All these, it may be safely assumed, were warranted primarily at the request of members of the forces, as most certainly was the Excelsior Encampment of 1860 to 1886, mentioned in chapter 7. The lists at Appendices H to J well illustrate the way in which the Orders spread to other countries.

It can be clearly understood from this that, until the nineteenth century was more than half over, the only practical source of the chivalric degrees in many places abroad would have been a Craft lodge or a Royal Arch chapter and these would often be held under the travelling warrant of a British regiment.

Canada

The first Grand Conclave warrant for Knights Templar in Canada was issued in 1824 to Hugh de Payens Encampment. Nineteen more followed in due course and, in 1875, they were to form the Great Priory of Canada and were removed from the English register. The Red Cross degree has been introduced from the United States, although that of Malta continues to follow the Templar working, and these are closer to our own. A photograph of some twenty years ago depicts the then Grand Master wearing a mantle and a cocked hat but it could be that more recent regulations have restored the more suitable Templar cap.

India and Elsewhere

By 1800, Lodge Humility with Fortitude (now No. 229 and working in London) was conferring the chivalric degrees at Fort William in Calcutta. The lodge had been warranted by the premier Grand Lodge in 1773 but, after an uncertain early career, had seceded to the Antients in 1798 as a stationary lodge for the Royal Artillery. A half-century later, and far to the north-west at Ambala in the Punjab, a Royal Arch chapter was working 'Ark and Mark, Super-Excellent, Red Cross Knight of Babylon and Templar degrees'. By this time, however, St. Augustine's Encampment was being established not too far away in Lahore and most if not all of its founders would have been previously knighted in a Craft or Royal Arch setting.

Soon after, as we can see from the evocative annual *Masonic Registers for India* published at this period, there were no fewer than eleven encampments in the country, and one each in Rangoon, Colombo and Singapore. Provincial Grand Conclaves existed for Bombay, Bengal and Burma but some encampments were directly under the Grand Conclave in London. As time went on there were to be additions to and subtractions from this tally as the members, military or civilian, were posted hither and thither.

With the granting of independence to India and Pakistan in 1947, the departure of British personnel reduced to a minimum or even to nil the number of Christian freemasons in most of the cities and cantonments. Some preceptories surrendered their warrants, amalgamating with others where this could be done, and — happily — others found it possible to transfer themselves to England. At the time of writing these words, only the Coromandel Preceptory

No. 73 of 1828 remains in India, at Madras, but in Sri Lanka two still meet as do preceptories in Singapore, Malaysia and Hong Kong.

Australasia

There is a complicated story to be told, but not here, about developments in Australia and New Zealand. The Percy Preceptory at Adelaide, dating from 1858, commands particular attention as having been warranted in the first place by Baldwyn, whose distinctive ritual (mentioned elsewhere) it has ever since used.

A curious incident toward the end of the 19th century was the forming of a 'Grand Priory of Victoria' by three preceptories which had been warranted by Canada. Rumblings in the corridors of power were silenced when the 'Grand Priory' came to an end, and two of the 'Canadian' preceptories were granted English warrants. There have been other occasions in the Antipodes when zealous but insufficiently expert brethren have tried to set up sovereign authorities for the Christian Orders. For instance, some fifteen years ago a 'Grand Priory of New Zealand Incorporated' came briefly on the scene.

More regularly, Scottish preceptories were also established in both countries and an Irish one in New Zealand; by the early 1980s, the United Orders were strongly represented there. The constitution in 1982 of the Great Priories of South Australia and Victoria, in 1984 of those of Western Australia and New South Wales, together with the United Great Priory of New Zealand, and in 1985 the Great Priory of Queensland, resulted in the transfer of allegiance of no fewer than eighty-two English preceptories to the new authorities. Many Scottish ones, with approval from Edinburgh, also exchanged their charters. One English preceptory remains at Darwin in Northern Australia.

Other Countries

The Liber Ordinis Templi of today lists the other English preceptories which are at work abroad, in South Africa, South America, Bermuda, the Caribbean and elsewhere. There are anecdotes in plenty about most of them, but here we can only repeat that there is evidence in many places of the earlier working of the Templar and Malta degrees by military or local lodges. F. W. Seal-Coon, in his admirable *Historical Account of Jamaican Freemasonry* (1976) refers to an 'Encampment No 13' (but on which roll?) as having been constituted in the island prior to 1794, but this cannot be traced in the records of the period in Great Priory's archives. The author then goes on to say that 'No 13' presumably worked within the Royal Lodge (now No. 207) at Kingston, which had from 1789 an Irish warrant, obtaining an English one in 1794. This lodge is known to have issued a Knight Templar certificate in 1800, while under the premier Grand Lodge.

District Chancellors

Since we are in the West Indies, it might be appropriate to mention a provision which was in the Statutes of Great Priory for quite a while — certainly from 1923 to 1948. It authorized the appointment, in Dominions and Dependencies of the British Crown, of a District Chancellor to supervise such preceptories as might be placed within his care. (In 1921 the United Grand Lodge had introduced Grand Inspectors for groups of lodges insufficient in number to justify the establishment of a District Grand Lodge, and from 1927 the Grand Inspectors were given rank in Grand Lodge; upon this innovation the District Chancellor's office was clearly based, although it did not carry with it a specific rank in Great Priory.) Only in two instances was such an appointment made: for the Bermudas, where there were and still are two preceptories, and for an area comprehensively described as 'British Guiana, Barbados, Trinidad and the Leeward Islands' although only the first two named possessed one preceptory each. After a few years the idea was abandoned although the relevant Statute remained for another twenty. The preceptories concerned then returned to direct administration from Great Priory.

Europe

Let us finally, in this chapter, take note of more recent developments in Europe, firstly those in which our own Great Priory has played a significant part.

In 1969 was consecrated the Olivier-de-la-Marche Preceptory No. 417 at Leiden in Holland. Seven others have since been founded there and, in 1983, a Provincial Prior was appointed for the Netherlands. In Finland, on the other hand, three preceptories, Alpha, Beta and Gamma, having been warranted from London in 1983 and 1984, these formed themselves into a sovereign Great Priory which our Grand Master constituted for them at Helsinki in 1985.

The Great Priory of Scotland was responsible for the establishment in recent years of the Great Priories of Germany and Greece. One of the eight German preceptories meets in Arabia, where the German Craft has been introduced.

The relationship which our Great Priory enjoys with the National Grand Lodges of the Scandinavian countries, with one of the German Grand Lodges and with the Grand Priories of Helvetia, France and Belgium will be discussed in the next chapter.

17

THE SCANDINAVIAN AND RECTIFIED SCOTTISH RITES

It is now time to look at some more of the 'bodies in amity' which are, in one or two instances not quite accurately, described in our *Liber Ordinis Templi* as 'other Great Priories'. Three of those currently listed practise what may be termed 'the Scandinavian Rite', while others adhere to the Rectified Scottish Rite.

The Scandinavian Rite

The Grand Lodge of Sweden and the National Grand Lodge of Denmark, who exchange representatives with our Great Priory, and the Grand Lodges of Norway and Iceland work in the Scandinavian (or Swedish) Rite as does the *Grosse Landesloge der Freimaurer von Deutschland*. It is essentially a ten-degree system.

In 'St. John's lodges' are worked the three Craft degrees; in St. Andrew's lodges the fourth, fifth and sixth are conferred. By agreement with Grand Chapters, including that of England, Royal Arch companions are welcome to visit St. Andrew's lodges up to the sixth degree, while brethren of the Scandinavian Rite who have attained the sixth degree may attend Royal Arch chapters. The right of intervisitation arises from the level reached in the respective systems, for there is no similarity between the rituals worked.

The higher degrees, in the Scandinavian countries, are conferred in Provincial Lodges, or by the Grand Lodge, and it is at this level that relationships with Great Priories of the Temple and Supreme Councils of the Ancient and Accepted Rite exist on a practical basis. For the latter, arrangements have existed since 1975 under which it is possible for members of the 18th, 30th and superior degrees to exchange visits with their Scandinavian brethren at specified levels according to rank. Such visits need to be agreed in advance through the respective masonic authorities.

There is no comparable rule under which a Knight Templar could expect to be able to pay such a visit. There are philosophical links between our ceremonial and that of the higher degrees in Scandinavia, but it has not been possible to establish a standing arrangement. However, brethren from either side who are genuinely interested in witnessing the relevant ceremonies of the other jurisdiction may request introductions, well in advance, through the proper channels. It is understood that sympathetic consideration would be given and that, subject to an obligation of secrecy, an invitation might be forthcoming.

While it is, of course, impossible to describe in these pages precisely how the ritual imparts the philosophical links, it could perhaps be mentioned that Jacques de Molay figures in the legend and that the candidate goes through a process of being armed and clothed.

The German Grand Lodge

In 1979 recognition by Great Priory was accorded to the *Grosse Landesloge* as the governing body of the Scandinavian Rite, and the foregoing observations may be taken to apply, *mutatis mutandis,* to relationships with this 'body in amity'. It ought to be explained that the *Grosse Landesloge* is one of the five authorities which constitute the 'United Grand Lodges of Germany' and that the other four work – in their different ways – only the three Craft degrees.

The Rectified Scottish Rite

The Grand Priory of Helvetia (Switzerland) and the *Grandes Prieurés de Galles* (France) *et Belgique,* who are also listed as 'other Great Priories', work according to the Rectified Scottish Rite. This is nominally a six-degree system but, as with the Ancient and Accepted Rite, the first three are regarded as having been conferred in a candidate's Craft lodge. There is a long and most interesting history of this rite, which was derived from the Rite of Strict Observance which has been more fully described in chapter 3. That story cannot be told here but it should be mentioned that the mother Grand Priory, that of Helvetia, dates from 1779.

The fourth degree of the system is in two parts, Scottish Master of St. Andrew and Perfect Master of St. Andrew. It is noteworthy that in Switzerland and France, where some of the regular lodges work the Craft degrees of the Rectified Scottish Rite, there are St. Andrew's lodges in which the rite is taken a stage further, and it is from these that the candidate moves onward.

The fifth degree of Novice leads into the last, *Chevalier Bienfaisant de la Cité Sainte* (Knight Beneficent of the Holy City), by which title the rite is often identified and can, like the Orders of the Temple and Malta, be seen to have a link with the medieval knights of Jerusalem.

There are today Grand Priories of the Rite in the United States (1934), France (1935), England (1937), Germany (1959) and, of more recent date, Belgium. That of England exists within the Great Priory of the United Orders and convenes but rarely. An independent commandery of the rite also exists in this country but its provenance is open to question. It is understood that English Knights Templar are received as visitors in French priories of the rite.

18

KNIGHT TEMPLAR PRIESTS

ALTHOUGH IT HAS no official connection with the United Orders of today, the Grand College of Holy Royal Arch Knight Templar Priests of Great Britain and Tabernacles Overseas deserves, on several counts, a place in this book. It is — for instance — the only regular masonic organization in England ('regular' in the sense that no objection to it has been raised by Grand Lodges and Chapters, or by any of the authorities centred upon Mark Masons' Hall) which requires its candidates to be Knights Templar; they must also be installed Masters in the Craft.

There are also historical links which cannot here be pursued in depth. It is, however, interesting to note among the degrees worked under the Irish Early Grand Encampment, already described, and the Early Grand Rite in Scotland (which has not as such so far been discussed, but also included those of the Temple and Malta) several which now survive only in the list of thirty-one 'Appendant Degrees' which are communicated by name to a Knight Templar Priest.

In the Eighteenth Century

The one degree which is now conferred in full crops up under various names and within several rites from the eighteenth century onwards. As 'White Mason' it took its place in the spectrum of blue, red, green and black within which the Craft, Royal Arch or Rose Croix, Red Cross and Templar degrees are sometimes named. There are traces in many of the English encampments in the 1780s and within the York Grand Lodge. There then followed a period of inactivity.

Nineteenth-Century Developments

From 1812 there was at Newcastle-upon-Tyne a Council of Knights Grand Cross of the Holy Temple of Jerusalem which included among its degrees that of Knight Templar Priest. This seems to have operated throughout the century until 1894 when the sole survivor admitted nine members of the Royal Kent Preceptory as Knight Templar Priests. Conscious, no doubt of the difficulties of continuing as an independent body, the revived body adhered to the Grand Council of the Allied Masonic Degrees which had been formed in London in 1880. It was to retain a measure of self-government but its activities seem to have been very limited for a number of years.

The Grand College is Formed

A significant point in the history was the admission as Knight Templar Priest of Colonel C. W. Napier-Clavering in 1913. When he became Grand Master of the Allied Degrees in 1920 he encouraged a change, already in train, by which the Newcastle 'Tabernacle' formed itself into a Grand College and took over from the Allied Degrees' Grand Council in 1923 or 1924 (there is some doubt as to the operative date) the control of the Knight Templar Priests. By 1930 seven more tabernacles had been constituted, one of them in New Zealand from which came the knight priests who, in 1933, established a regular and sovereign Grand College in the United States. There followed in England some years of 'consolidation' but in the 1940s began an expansion which has continued. Of more than 140 tabernacles now working, many are in Commonwealth countries and South Africa, and there are others in the Netherlands and Germany. It is interesting to find that in recent times one has been formed at Edinburgh.

Whereas all other masonic degrees and Orders emanating from England have always been administered from London, the Grand College of Knight Templar Priests has had its seat in the north, for long at Newcastle but now at York.

19

OTHER ORDERS AND SOCIETIES

FINALLY WE TURN to a number of organizations having a Templar connotation but no relationship whatever with the regular masonic Order of the Temple. (Some which are or were predicated upon the medieval Hospitallers and their successors have been brought to notice in chapter 2 and Fabré-Palaprat's Order is dealt with at Appendix A.)

Prince Hall Freemasonry

It is proper to mention firstly the Prince Hall fraternity centred upon the United States but extending its influence to many other countries. This is not the place to discuss its history; suffice it to say that it has long provided a structure of Freemasonry for the worthy coloured gentlemen who have in general been ineligible for admission to the American system which we regard as regular. In certain of the States Negro brethren have long enjoyed membership of what, for the sake of clarity, may be termed 'regular' lodges; under the Grand Lodge of New Jersey there has been for well over a century a lodge consisting entirely of such brethren. There has been ongoing dialogue for many years, largely in the northern states, between the leaders of the 'white' and Negro Grand Lodges and this has borne fruit in at least one State where very recently the two fraternities have entered into formal relationship and intervisitation is now permissible.

The Prince Hall organization has long modelled itself upon that of the 'regulars', to the extent that it includes the Royal Arch and the United Orders, together with the Ancient and Accepted (Scottish) Rite and sundry other degrees. It follows, therefore, that on their own great occasions coloured Knights Templar march as bravely in the streets as do those of the regular Grand Commanderies. There is no reason to doubt that in due course more barriers will be removed and that, in those States where a more relaxed attitude prevails, the privilege of intervisitation will be extended beyond the Craft lodges.

It must be emphasized that there are several other 'masonic' societies existing primarily for Negroes which are acceptable neither to the regular Grand Lodges nor to those of the Prince Hall fraternity.

'Fringe Masonry'

In a somewhat mysterious area, and we will not explore it too thoroughly, there have been instances in which the words 'Templar' or 'Temple' have been included in the titles of quasi-masonic bodies which have appeared upon the scene, usually for a limited period. In Germany, for example, an extraordinary character named Theodor Reuss included among numerous 'fringe' activities his 'Order of the Temple of the Orient'. This story belongs to the early years of this century and it will be sufficient to mention that the Head of the Order in England was none other than Aleister Crowley, whose wide interests included what may be loosely described as 'black magic'. (Those who wish to know more about this are referred to a splendid paper on Reuss, by Ellic Howe and Helmut Möller, in *AQC* 91, 1978.)

The degree of 'Knight of the Temple' which was included in the Ancient and Primitive Rite, and which is, under varying titles, the 27th of the Ancient and Accepted (Scottish) Rite, is more directly concerned with King Solomon's Temple and not with the medieval knights.

The Prieuré de Sion

In 1982 was published *The Holy Blood and the Holy Grail* by Michael Baigent, Richard Leigh and Henry Lincoln, which one reviewer described as 'a mystic drop too much'. The authors would have us believe that the medieval Knights Templar were the military and executive arm of the Prieuré de Sion, which was, it seems, a secret organization. Those who wish to know more of this remarkable and, it must be admitted, highly readable, story must turn to their book, but — by way of an appetizer — let us note here that the Prieuré is reported to have carried on when the Templars were suppressed. Its Grand Masters in more recent times are said to have included Isaac Newton, Victor Hugo, Claude Debussy and

Cocteau. One is inevitably reminded of the apocryphal list of Grand Masters ascribed to the Craft by James Anderson and others; it begins with Moses!

The Good Templars

The 'Good Templars' were — and possibly still are — a society of total abstainers. It seems unlikely that it would have claimed kinship with the knights of old, who probably enjoyed their goblets of wine or ale, especially at an era when the quality and taste of drinking water often left much to be desired.

20
MISCELLANY

THERE ARE COLLECTED here a few points which have arisen in the course of research but do not readily fit into the pattern of the previous chapters.

Lodge Names

Most lodges bearing the name 'Temple', or having that word in their titles, will associate themselves with King Solomon's Temple. Obvious exceptions are those called 'Temple Bar' and another is possible for Temple Fortune, so-called after a village now incorporated in Hendon, where some knights might have been established in their day. Lodges named 'Templar' (Calcutta) and 'Templars' (London) seem to have had a connection with the temperance movements.

Much more interesting is the Knights of Malta Lodge, now No. 50, at Hinckley in Leicestershire, which was warranted by the Antient Grand Lodge in 1803 and is likely to have worked, for a few years, in the Templar, Malta and Rose Croix degrees.

No less worthy of consideration is the Knight of Malta Lodge (this time in the singular), again of the Antients, which had a travelling warrant – also issued in 1803 – in the 2nd Royal Lancashire Militia. It lasted only until about 1814 but is recorded as having worked successively in the counties of Durham, Essex, Northumberland, Lancashire, Yorkshire and Devonshire. As with the Hinckley lodge, this too could have conferred the Royal Arch and chivalric degrees.

Lastly, under this heading, is to be mentioned the very brief use of the name of Ancient Knight Templars' Lodge No. 53 of the Antients, dating – despite its number – only from 1809. In the following year it became Humber Lodge and as No. 57 it continues to meet at Hull. A relationship to the Antient York Conclave of Redemption, which moved from York to Hull and was there said to have met 'within the Minerva Lodge' (now No. 250), can be ruled out as that move took place many years later.

The Military Lodges' Preceptory No 300

This title deserves some explanation. At the end of the last war, three of the Irish travelling military lodges, St. Patrick's in the 4th/7th Royal Dragoon Guards, Charity in the 5th Royal Inniskilling Dragoon Guards and Leswarree in the Queen's Royal Irish Hussars, were often meeting at Mark Masons' Hall in London. This continued for several years, although it was occasionally possible for a lodge to convene within its regiment, in England or overseas. Several of the brethren who were active in these lodges who were already members of the United Orders obtained in 1945 a warrant for a preceptory to meet in London. Happily it continues to do so; less fortunate were Charity and Leswarree Lodges, for they had eventually to close down. St. Patrick survives, as does one other travelling lodge, Glittering Star in the Worcestershire and Sherwood Foresters' Regiment. They both date from the eighteenth century, when they are known to have worked the Templar and Malta degrees.

For Knights Philatelic

'Thematic' stamp collectors who are members of the United Orders would be able to assemble several albums of stamps and covers which would reflect much of history covered in this book. The issues of Malta and Rhodes, for instance, would be a rewarding source. Masonic first day covers from America may well include some of interest to us.

Less generally known is that the Sovereign Order of Malta has issued its own series of stamps, and these can be obtained through certain dealers in this country or, of course, at the Order's *Palazzo Magistrale* in Rome. Some of the commemorative series are especially interesting: there was one in 1967 depicting the standards of the Grand Master and the *langues,* another in 1972 showing the fortresses of the Hospitallers, and two in 1974 portraying the cardinal and theological virtues.

Albert Edward, Prince of Wales

In 1938, Leonard Forsyth produced for Faith and Fidelity Preceptory No. 26 of London an excellent little history to mark the centenary of the Warrant of Confirmation. This was one of a number which, in earlier days, used the term 'Early Grand Encampment of England' as part of their titles.

The preceptory is rightly proud of the fact that the Prince of Wales, almost immediately after his appearance in Grand Conclave in 1870, accepted honorary membership. In 1872 he was installed as Eminent Commander, in which office he remained until he ascended the throne as King Edward VII, when he became Patron of the preceptory. In connection with this change, a letter from a senior member to the King's Private Secretary stated, *inter alia,* that – as Prince – he had been installed *as a member of the Order* [author's italics] in the preceptory in 1870. Had this been so the history would have reproduced the Minutes of the occasion!

The occasion of 1872 was thus reported in *The North British Daily Mail:*

> His Royal Highness the Prince of Wales attended on Monday afternoon at the great hall in the Freemasons' Tavern, Great Queen Street, for the purpose of being installed a brother of the 'Faith and Fidelity' Lodge of Good Templars. The public by some means became aware of the intended visit and a large number of persons assembled to witness the arrival of the prince, who was loudly cheered as he drove up in a private carriage.

We can forgive the untutored assumption that the Prince was entering the Order, rather than arising within it, but the Prince himself might not have forgiven the implication that he had 'signed the pledge' of a teetotaller!

Some Cornish By-laws

Reposing in the archives, but not hitherto mentioned, is a beautifully engrossed manuscript copy, sumptuously bound in red leather, of 'The Bye-Laws of the Holy Sacred Royal Exalted Religious and Military Order of H.R.D.M. Grand Elected Masonic Knights Templars Hospitalers and of Malta K.D.S.H. Saint John of Jerusalem Palastine Rhodes &c No.3'. This rather attenuated title (the spelling is as in the original) does not reveal that the laws were those of St. John of Jerusalem Encampment of Redruth, warranted by Grand Conclave in January 1792.

The by-laws were approved and confirmed in 1817 and signed by all present but the only name here to be mentioned is that of the formidable John Knight, 'M.E.G.M.', whose firm hand then governed the chivalric Orders of the Duchy of Cornwall. One or two of the rules, which were undoubtedly devised by him, are quoted here because they reveal something of the procedure, as distinct from ceremonial. It is not difficult to imagine the scene at Pearce's Hotel at one of the meetings which, by modern standards, were frequent indeed:

> Conclave held on 2nd Wednesday in every month and on 11 March in every year precisely at 12 noon. Dinner on the table at 3 o'clock. Bill called and Conclave closed at 8 in the evening precisely.
>
> The M.E.G.M. may, as in times past, convene a Conclave or Counsel [*sic*] of a Chapter as often as he shall have occasion to do so.
>
> No member or visiting companion can be admitted without his Apron, Sash, Star, and Cross of the Order.
>
> No one may call for any liquor to be brought into the Conclave without the express orders of the Most Eminent Grand Master.
>
> That it shall be incumbent upon the First Captain to remind the M.E.G.M. of the hour of 8 if a dinner or the hour of 10 if an evening Conclave, who shall immediately proceed to close the Conclave, as nothing can be more conducive than well timed meetings to the Peace, Honour and Harmony of the Conclave, to our Health, and to the Satisfaction of our Relations and Families at Home.

The Knights Companions of those days clearly expected to spend rather longer at the festive board that we generally do today, and one wonders whether the 'Relations and Families at Home' were wholly satisfied about the arrangements'!

Vice-Chancellors and Chancelleries

There is some difficulty in identifying the worthy knights who, did the early paper-work of the Orders. Thomas Dunckerley in his day carried out a good deal of the necessary correspondence from Hampton Court. The loss by fire in 1820, at the house of the Vice-Chancellor, Robert Gill, of most of the records suggests that he had been 'working from home'. In July 1807 he published the Grand Conclave Minutes from No. 40 Bishopgate Without; by October he had moved to 16 Sun Street, Bishopsgate Without and was still there in 1812.

Burckhardt, the Deputy Grand Master, was 'holding the Order together' during the decidedly inactive period up to 1830, and probably ran much of the business thereafter at his own expense as he was 'out of pocket' when he was at last able to give up. Later Vice-Chancellors may well have used their business-places as the Orders' offices. The 'Chancellerie' from which a manuscript ritual was issued in 1871 (*see* chapter 13) was at 14 Bedford Row, not very far from Red Lion Square whither Grand Mark Lodge, formed in

1856, had moved in 1867. In 1890 this was able to move into its first real home at Mark Masons' Hall, Great Queen Street (formerly Bacon's Hotel). Charles F. Matier had in the previous year become Grand Secretary of the Mark and was already or would be in comparable office in the other degrees and Orders whose administration has since then been centred upon the Mark headquarters. When, in 1896, he was appointed Great Vice-Chancellor in the United Orders it was logical and convenient for the Chancellery to move in also and – in successive Mark Masons' Halls at 71 Kingsway, 40 Upper Brook Street and now 86 St. James's Street – there it has remained.

The Mark Grand Secretary is always our Great Vice-Chancellor and holds also the highest secretarial offices in the Order of the Red Cross of Constantine, the Royal and Select Masters, the Allied Masonic Degrees, and the Order of the Secret Monitor.

Meeting Places

Again we are absolved by the scarcity of records from positive statements as to where the Grand Conclave held all its early meetings. We do know that the inaugural convocation was at the Unicorn Tavern, which is most likely to have been the one of that name in Covent Garden. It is also on record that in 1806 and 1807 St. Paul's Coffee House, in St. Paul's Churchyard, was the venue, but the available Minutes for some time after inform us that Grand Conclave was convening at Freemasons' Tavern, on the site of the present Freemasons' Hall, Great Queen Street. An analysis of the existing records would no doubt enable a full list for the rest of the century to be drawn up but it would be tedious and time-consuming to attempt this.

The records which have been quoted of the few gatherings of the Convent General indicate the use of non-masonic accommodation but – once the Mark Masons' Hall of 1890 came into being – Great Priory regularly met there. When the lease ran out in 1939 and everything moved to 71 Kingsway, where the lodge rooms were small, and again when 40 Upper Brook Street was acquired in 1954, the great occasions of the various Orders had to be held elsewhere. For many years the large subterranean temple at the Café Royal accommodated the annual convocations of the two Great Priories but from 1977 onwards we have met at Freemasons' Hall, Great Queen Street, where the Grand Temple has provided a splendid setting for the assembled knights and our ceremonial has been seen to the best possible advantage.

Appendix A

THE CHARTER OF LARMENIUS

This large parchment — sometimes described as the *Charta Transmissionis* — was presented to Great Priory in about 1911 by F. J. W. Crowe, a distinguished masonic scholar who had been Master of Quatuor Coronati Lodge in 1909-10. Only on its acquisition had he discovered it to be the original of a document which had long been the subject of controversy and which, even today, is believed by some to prove the lineal descent of masonic Knights Templar, through a succession of Grand Masters, from Jacques de Molay who was executed in 1314 (*see* chapter 1).

Crowe, before relinquishing the charter, examined it minutely, transcribing from the cipher in which the Latin text is concealed, and comparing his version thereof with that given by C. A. Thory in *Acta Latomorum* (1815). He then translates the Latin, which by successive signatures (that of John Mark Larmenius being the first), takes the 'transmission' from 1324 to 1804, and also the endorsements in French which are dated in 1812.

These transcriptions and translations were published in an admirable paper in *Ars Quatuor Coronatorum* (the transactions of Quatuor Coronati Lodge), volume 24 (1911), which includes excellent illustrations of the charter and other documents. The author reproduces in full the reasons put forward by J. G. Findel (*History of Freemasonry*, 1866, page 717) for condemning the charter as spurious. He also gives the Abbé F. G. Bègue Clavel's story, written in 1844, of its alleged fabrication in 1705.

Crowe sought the opinion of the then Keeper of Manuscripts at the British Museum, an acknowledged expert, who was satisfied that the text was in the Latin of the 14th century (which Findel had doubted) but found that its illuminations were typical of a period which did not begin until the late 15th century. By their nature they could not have been superimposed on an already existing text.

Many years later in 1966, G. E. W. Bridge wrote:

> I understand that the British Museum have recently examined it again and are of the opinion that the inks employed do not accord with all the alleged dates [that is, of the added signatures]. I wish I knew when that particular cypher was first used — I have found no evidence but suspect a later date — probably post-1740.

One important and obvious flaw in the charter is that it lacks the signature of de Molay himself, from whom the supposed transmission of authority must necessarily proceed. This has to be taken into account before acknowledging or disproving all or any of the endorsements of those shown as having accepted Grand Mastership down to 1804. We cannot here go into the arguments as to why this gap could be overlooked; the fact that de Molay was already dead when the document is claimed to have been drawn up would not, to a critical historian, forgive the author of it for assuming the authority of a Grand Master. It must also be said that the Grand Mastership of the Templars had always been an elective office and this too invalidates the accession of Larmenius and those who are reputed to have succeeded him.

In the context of the present volume, the masonic Knights Templar of today must wonder how they are linked to the year 1804, and here we are in difficulty. We have learned in chapter 2 that our earliest-known masonic predecessors had come on the scene several decades previously. The presumption has been made that we might reasonably trace our origins through the Strict Observance, also an eighteenth-century source. It had therefore to be admitted that, whether it be true or false, the Charter of Larmenius does nothing to establish *our* ancestry!

The heirs to the transmission, through Bernard Raymund Fabré (1777-1838; elsewhere known as Fabré-Palaprat), the last Grand Master named in the charter, seem to have been the members of *another* Order of the Temple. Palaprat was both a doctor of medicine and a prelate in one of many rather tiny and ephemeral Christian churches. Presumably on the strength of the Larmenius document, he was also the Grand Master of this Order from 1804 to 1813 and again — after a short period out of office — until his death. He is accused (Peter Anson, *Bishops at Large*, 1964, page 301) of having fabricated the charter and also several relics of de Molay and others to lend authenticity to his appointment, a view shared by Clavel.

In our Great Priory's archives there are some interesting relics of this Order, which appears to have been non-masonic but which had in membership some very eminent and influential freemasons of the day, including the royal Dukes of Kent and Sussex, and the Dukes of Leinster and Atholl,[1] the last-named being the Grand Master in 1848. The Duke of Leeds was at that time appointed Grand Preceptor of England. This is not the place further to pursue the Order's history. Traces of it may survive but in all probability it ran out of steam and, with it, the claimed line of succession to the Charter of Larmenius.

[1] The sixth of the line, who ruled the Scottish Craft from 1843 to 1864 and the Royal Grand Conclave from 1845 to 1863.

Appendix B

STATUTES, 1791

The flourishing state of *Symbolic* MASONRY, under the protection of his Royal Highness the PRINCE OF WALES, Grand Master; and the great increase of *Royal Arch* Chapters, patronized by his Royal Highness the DUKE OF CLARENCE; having animated the masonic KNIGHTS TEMPLARS of ST. JOHN OF JERUSALEM, &c. with a desire to revive their ancient, royal, exalted, religious, and military order; they confederated and unanimously selected their brother and knight companion, *Thomas Dunckerley,* of Hampton Court Palace, in the county of Middlesex, Grand Master of the confraternity, under the patronage of his Royal Highness PRINCE EDWARD, T.H.E.

1791, at London, on the Feast of St. John the Baptist, a grand and royal conclave was held; when the following *ancient* statutes of the order were *revised* and *enacted*:

The public interests of the confraternity of knights templars, as a collective body, are to be regulated by a general convocation of all the chapters of encampment on record; or by their representatives, the respective eminent and captains, commanding columns; who, with the most eminent and supreme grand master of the order, attended by his grand officers, compose the grand and royal *chapter*.

The grand and royal conclave or council of the order, is to consist of the grand master and officers, with the three principals of every chapter.

The high office of grand master is held during his natural life, or until such time, as for particular reason he shall signify his intention to resign.

On the death or resignation of a grand master, the acting grand master is to summon a convocation of the order, who are to select or elect another most eminent and supreme grand master; and at the first convenient opportunity he is to be proclaimed in the *ancient manner* at a *proper place*.

The grand master is to appoint all the grand officers, except the treasurer who is to be elected annually in the grand and royal chapter.

On a vacancy of grand patron of the order, the grand master is to make humble suit, in the name of the confraternity, to a prince of the blood-royal of Great Britain (if a knight of the order) requesting his patronage.

The grand master by his authority may appoint provincial acting grand masters for districts at a distance from the grand metropolis.

A grand and royal chapter is to be convoked annually on the Feast of St. John the Baptist, in the grand field of encampment, at London. The solemnity of the day is to begin with the public worship of the Grand Architect of the universe, and by making offerings for the poor. An exhortation is to be given by the grand orator. The grand officers are to be appointed by the grand master for the ensuing year. The knights companions are to eat the bread of thankfulness, and drink the cup of chearfulness with their grand officers.

Every regular conclave or chapter of encampment is to be constituted by patent, with the seal of the order, under the sign-manual of the grand master, and witnessed by the acting grand master, grand chancellor, and grand scribe and register; for which one pound and six shillings is to be paid, or a sum equal to the fee for installing a knight in the chapter. For as all chapters have authority to make bye laws and regulations, for the good government of the same, provided they are conformable to these antient statutes, they may enact any sum for the installation of a knight templar, not less than one pound and six shillings.

Every knight companion of the order is to be registered in the grand and royal conclave at London; for which five shillings is to be paid; and a certificate of his register will be delivered or sent to him, and signed with the seal of the grand master, by the second scribe.

According to ancient custom, a complete chapter of the order is to consist of an *eminent* deputy grand master, two captains commanding columns, two standard-bearers with knights attendants, and one or two equeries*.

The conclave or council of a chapter is to consist of the five principal officers above mentioned, with the treasurer and scribe.

On all ballots for admission of candidates, *one* black ball is to exclude. The eminent deputy grand master of a chapter is to be elected annually on the feast of St. John the divine, by a majority of the knights; and he is to appoint the other officers, except the treasurer, who is to be elected by the officers and knights companions of the chapter.

The name of the eminent grand master of a chapter, when elected, is to be sent to the most eminent and supreme grand master.

If a knight should present himself at any conclave or chapter without his sash and medal, with the distinctive marks of the order, he shall not take a seat, or fill any office in that conclave or chapter; unless (for reasons assigned) a dispensation is granted by the eminent D.G.M.

Every knight is to remember, that our ancient and royal order is founded on the love of God, benevolence to mankind, and charity to the poor and distressed, the sick and wounded; therefore, after the prayer, (at the opening of the chapter) the poor's-box is to be presented to very knight companion.

The knights companions are to keep with the greatest care the secrets of their election, and work assiduously in the reformation of their morals; never to lose sight of the *mysterious steps* they have taken; but endeavour to exercise the duties they contain, by a strict fidelity to the grand master, and to the order. They are to reconcile differences between their brethren; not to speak without permission from the eminent D.G.M. after the prayer and opening of the chapter. They are to pay due attention to the working; not to laugh or joke, or behave unseemly. If a knight neglect to attend his proper chapter after having been duly summoned, he shall be fined according to the Bye-Laws of the said chapter.

The knights in general are to distinguish themselves from the rest of mankind, by their most intimate and perfect union; by their readiness to relieve their brethren in distress, and procuring for them all the happiness in their power.

The standards are to be placed on each side the throne; and are not to be taken out of the chapter, but on particular occasions, by permission from the M.E.& S. grand master.

Every knight is to write his name on the lower corner of his certificate or register for *particular* reasons, well known to the confraternity; and he is to produce the same on his first visit to a regular constituted chapter, where none are to be admitted but those who are registered in the grand and royal conclave, except knights companions from foreign chapters.

Every chapter is to assemble on the 11th day of March annually, to humble themselves before the Great Disposer of all events, with fasting and prayer; and to make their offerings for the poor and needy.

Any subject which is not treated of in the aforegoing statutes must be decided by the general rules of masonry, contained in the book of constitutions.

The above laws were read at a grand conclave, June 24th , 1791, and were unanimously approved of.

NOTE: In reproducing the text of the Constitutions, the original spelling and typography have been followed throughout, with the exception of the then customary alternative form of the letter 's'.

* Janitor or Tyler.

Appendix C

THE CHARTER OF CONSTITUTION, 1809

His Royal Highness Prince Edward Duke of Kent
Knight of the Most Honorable [*sic*] and Illustrious Orders of the Garter and St. Patrick, &c., &c., &c.

To the Knights Companions of the Exalted Religious and Military Orders of the Holy Temple and Sepulchre and of St. John of Jerusalem HRDM KDSH

HEALTH PEACE GOODWILL

WHEREAS certain of our Brethren being Knights Companions of the said Religious and Military Order viz[t] James Higgins MD, Robert Gill, Evan Lloyd, John Gilbert, William Davis, James Murray and John R Saffell did heretofore present to us their humble Suit and Petition stating that the antient Grand Conclave of the said Order had for many Years suspended and discontinued its Meetings and that the Members thereof were for the most part dead or dispersed without hope of them being again assembled to resume the exercise of their former Functions and Privileges and praying that we would be pleased to grant unto them our Charter for the purpose of constituting and forming them into a Supreme Grand Conclave of the said Order AND WHEREAS we in Consideration of the Premises did grant unto them such Charter as aforesaid bearing date the – day of March in the year of our Lord One thousand eight hundred and four therein and thereby enacting and declaring such Constitutions as upon their representation we considered advisable AND WHEREAS since the time above mentioned the Officers and Members of the Grand Conclave Successors of our said Brethren and Knights Companions have found and discovered certain Constitutions made and agreed upon in the Year of our Lord One thousand seven hundred and ninety one under the Grand Mastership of our late Brother and Knight Companion Sir Thomas Dunckerley now deceased by the Officers and Members of the Grand Conclave at that time existing in strict conformity with the antient Constitutions and usages of the Order of Knights Templars from time immemorial AND WHEREAS they have represented to us that the said Charter and the Constitutions therein contained are in many respects inconsistent with and repugnant to such antient Constitutions and usages and have humbly besought us to revoke cancel and annul the same granting unto them a new Charter in all things consistent therewith NOW KNOW YE THAT WE in consideration of such their humble Suit and Petition do hereby revoke cancel and annul our said Charter bearing date the said – day of March in the year of our Lord One thousand eight hundred and four and DO hereby ratify and confirm the said Constitutions bearing date the *24th* day of June in the year of our Lord One thousand seven hundred and ninety one in all things whatsoever save and except inasmuch as relates to the amount of the fees to be charged in Warrants of Constitution and Certificates to be hereafter granted to any Knights Companions of the said Order and the day on which the annual Grand Conclave and Festival of the said Order is appointed to be holden which matters so excepted are henceforth to be regulated by the discretion of the Grand Conclave for the time being AND in pursuance of the said Constitutions We DO hereby accept and take upon us the Style Title and Office of ROYAL GRAND PATRON of the said Order wherewith by the said Constitutions we are invested for the term of our Life AND WHEREAS it has seemed good to the Members of the Grand Conclave assembled in due form on Sunday the twelfth day of April in the year of our Lord One thousand eight hundred and seven to elect constitute and appoint our Brother and Knight Companion of the said Order Sir Waller Rodwell Wright to be Grand Master of the said Order for and during the term of his life and to invest him with all the Powers of the Office of Grand Master according to the said Constitutions belonging and appertaining KNOW YE FURTHER that we do hereby approve ratify and confirm the said election and appointment and do also confirm unto our said Brother and Knight Companion Waller Rodwell Wright all the Powers and Privileges of the said Office of Grand Master belonging and appertaining AND WE DO by these Presents further grant unto the said Sir Waller Rodwell Wright Grand Master of the said Order aforesaid And also Sir John Christian Burckhardt Deputy Grand Master, Sir Charles Valentine first Grand Captain, Sir Richard Jebb second Grand

Captain, The Reverend Sir John Frith DD Grand Prelate, *Sir William Henry White* Grand Chancellor, Sir Robert Gill Grand Register, Sir John Gilbert Grand Treasurer for the present Year in the possession and exercise of those several Offices actually being and generally to all other the acting Grand Officers of the said Order that they and their Successors Grand Master and Grand Officers of the said Order shall have and enjoy all Powers Privileges and Immunities to the Grand Master and Grand Officers of the said Order heretofore appertaining and shall together with the Representatives of such Chapters or Encampments of the said Order as do now or may hereafter legally exist in this Kingdom of Great Britain or so many of them as may be present hold four Grand Conclaves of the said Order in every Year at such intervals as shall by the said Grand Master and his Grand Officers for the time being be judged expedient for the purpose of enacting such Laws and Regulations as they may judge conducive to the Interests and wellbeing of the said Order not being repugnant to or inconsistent with antient Constitutions thereof inasmuch as the same are hereby confirmed and ratified and generally for deciding upon and determining all matters relative to the said Order.

IN WITNESS whereof we have hereunto affixed our Signature and Royal Seal this *Tenth day of April A.I. 5813 – A.S.H. 1809 A.O. 691 – A.Cod. 495*

[*signed*] Edward P

We the undersigned DO most thankfully accept the above Charter of Constitution acknowledging His Royal Highness Edward Duke of Kent to be lawfully and constitutionally the Royal Grand Patron of the said Order and promising strict conformity with all Constitutions Laws Ordinances and Regulations herein above approved ratified and confirmed

[*signed*]
Waller Rodwell Wright Grand Master
John Christian Burckhardt Dep.G.M.
Charles Davis Valentine First Grand Captain
Richard Jebb Second Grand Captain
John Frith G.Prelate
W.H. White Grand Chancellor
Robert Gill G.V. Chancellor & Reg^{r}
John Gilbert G.Treasurer

NOTES 1 The date in March 1804 of the Duke of Kent's earlier Charter, not entered in this one, was the 18th. The document was not signed until nearly another year had passed, at the meeting of Grand Conclave on 11 March 1805. (Matier, *The Origin and Progress of the Preceptory of St. George*, 1910)

2 The Charter is engrossed but certain details, here printed in *italics*, were added in handwriting after engrossment

Appendix D

THE END OF THE CONVENT GENERAL, 1895

The Grand Master's Declaration

WHEREAS at an Ordinary Meeting of Convent General of the United Religious and Military Orders of the Temple and of St. John of Jerusalem, Palestine, Rhodes and Malta, holden at the Mark Masons Hall, Great Queen Street on Friday the 11 May 1894 it was resolved to appoint a Commission to enquire into the relations existing between the National Great Priories and Convent General.

AND WHEREAS the Commission reported that the objects sought to be effected by the Institution of Convent General have not been attained and that the Institution itself is in no way calculated to promote the good of the Order. And that the National Great Priories of England and Wales and of Ireland have in consequence presented to us a Petition praying us to dissolve Convent General and to allow ourself to be named Sovereign of the Order in the United Kingdom.

AND WHEREAS such dissolution appears to Us to be for the benefit of the Order, and we have determined to give our assent thereto in manner hereafter appearing,

NOW WE ALBERT EDWARD, PRINCE OF WALES, K.G.,G.C.T., &c., &c., &c., &c., Grand Master of the said United Orders DO HEREBY in virture of the power vested in us, absolve the said National Great Priories of England and Wales and of Ireland from their allegiance to Convent General and do declare that the Convent General of the said United Orders shall from and after the date hereof cease to exist.

AND WE DO HEREBY consent to the request of the said National Great Priories that We should permit ourself to be named the Sovereign of the Order in the United Kingdom.

DONE at Marlborough House this
19th day of July, A.D. 1895, A.O. 777
[*signed*] Albert Edward
Grand Master

Appendix E

THE BALDWYN ENCAMPMENT

There must be included, in any history of the United Orders, more than a little about the beginnings, the development, the markedly independent attitude and the workings of what is variously described as 'The Camp of Baldwyn at Bristol', 'The Baldwyn Encampment' or — more often than not — just 'Baldwyn'. Although reference has been made to it in other parts of this book, it is but fair to Baldwyn to make clear that it has been for a great many years a most loyal and most highly valued division in the army of knights who serve under the direction of our Great Priory.

Like four other preceptories at the head of our roll (they too have the privilege of using more ancient styles) it is shown as 'Time Immemorial' and we ought to give a moment's thought to what that qualification conveys. To the uninstructed and popular world it usually confers a cachet of hoary antiquity, measurable in centuries if not millenia. To the freemason, however, 'Time Immemorial' after the name of a lodge, chapter, council or preceptory is intended only to show that it was in being before, if only by a year or so, its present sovereign authority was established.

The Beginning

We must bear in mind that our Great Priory originated in 1791, when a number of 'chapters or encampments' were brought together under Thomas Dunckerley. Baldwyn itself would not claim to have been formed more than a few years before 1780, and so it was still comparatively youthful when it accepted Dunckerley as its second ruler and then, with the others, recognized him as the Grand Master over all. We have several times mentioned the fact that the Templar and Malta degrees were being worked in lodges and chapters for some years before anyone thought of hiving them away into what became known as encampments. This is no less true of the situation in Bristol. Thomas Duckett's excellent account, *The Baldwyn Saga*, was written in 1980 to commemorate the bicentenary of a document which we shall soon be describing, and he tells us that Knights Templar were certainly meeting in Bristol in January 1772. If this were so, we must assume that they had acquired the degrees through Craft or Royal Arch channels, as would have been the case with the predecessors of any of the earliest encampments.

Thomas Duckett, who was Grand Superintendent of the Camp of Baldwyn from 1971 to 1976, does not give the evidence for that date of 1772 but it is likely to rest in a report in a local newspaper of 25 January in that year:

> A young recruiting party, Captain Turpentine, Lieutenant Sweet, Ensign Grogg, Sergeant House, Corporal Hemp and Drummer Guzzle . . . and then home to spend the evening under the Rose with the Knights Templar.

This has all the hallmarks of a skit and it seems doubtful that the more junior of the ranks were likely to have been acceptable for advancement to the chivalric degrees. But, in any event, the report cannot serve as *evidence* of a formal masonic meeting.

More acceptable are the Minutes of the Sea Captains' Lodge, mentioned in chapter 3, for 1783 but that first unimpeachable record is three years too late to be of use to Baldwyn. The importance to them of the year 1780 is that they treasure a 'Charter of Compact', claimed to have been drawn up in that year and signed by Joshua Springer (from whom Dunckerley took over in 1791) as Most Eminent Grand Master, and 'others on appointment to principal offices'. This was a 'self-generated' document; here were the local knights seeking to confirm the prior existence (from a date not specified in the document) of what they called 'The Supreme Grand and Royal Encampment of Knights Templar of St John of Jerusalem, Knights Hospitallers and Knights of Malta, etc., etc.' which is roughly what the knights elsewhere, and certainly the Grand Conclave, called themselves. Although we cannot now digest his arguments, Eric Ward ('The Baldwyn Rite – An Impartial Survey', *AQC* 71, 1958) raised doubts about the Charter, and gave reasons for suspecting in particular its date of 1780. Other than that document, all *internal* evidence prior to 1808 has disappeared; historians, including those from within Baldwyn have had to rely on other sources.

In the Charter, however, is a statute which includes:

> Be it therefore known that no Encampment within the Kingdom of England will be acknowledged by us, unless they admit of our Supremacy and conform to the Statutes . . .

which gives a distinct impression that they had visions of attracting Knights Templar in other parts of England and forming in due time a sovereign authority for the whole country. That hope was unfulfilled but from this statute very probably derived the strongly independent line which was, and indeed is, such a characteristic of Baldwyn.

Later Years

Although in 1791 Dunckerley had been able to take them into his Grand Conclave, the uncertainties of the period which followed his death left them unhappy about the association. By the simple device of resuming their previous independent status Baldwyn was able to carry on while the rest of the Order was inactive, but there were times when they appeared to be returning to the fold. For instance, when the Duke of Sussex became Grand Master in 1812 he allowed himself to be proposed for membership of Baldwyn, and Kemeys Tynte — who was to become Grand Master in 1846 — joined the encampment in 1829. But Baldwyn paid no annual dues to Grand Conclave throughout this period and until, in 1862 and after much negotiation, a very different sort of Charter of Compact brought them again, and permanently, under Grand Conclave.

In this charter there were, of course, firm undertakings on both sides, but the most important were that Baldwyn should have time immemorial status, should be permitted to continue with its own special ceremonial and that Bristol should be constituted as a Province of the Order. In 1960 a supplemental charter enshrined Baldwyn's right to nominate a brother knight for appointment as Provincial Prior for Bristol. It is well understood that the ruler of the Camp of Baldwyn — long entitled the 'Grand Superintendent' — shal be so nominated and that his Province shall nowadays consist only of the Baldwyn Encampment.

The same eminent brother, by a somewhat similar treaty in 1881 with the Supreme Council 33°, also takes office automatically as Inspector General for Bristol, with only the Baldwyn Rose Croix Chapter in his care.

The Seven Degrees of Baldwyn

We have mentioned elsewhere the close association of the Templar and Rose Croix degrees, which continued until the Supreme Council was established in 1845. To find the Rose Croix at Bristol today in a Baldwyn context is not therefore surprising. We must now recall that Baldwyn was a repository (and long the only one) of a rite of seven degrees and it still enjoys this unique responsibility, answering to Great Priory and the Supreme Council only for of the sixth and seventh respectively.

There is some little difficulty about the arithmetic when it comes to listing the seven:

1 The Craft (three degrees, ideally to have been taken in a Bristol lodge)
2 The Royal Arch (to be taken in one of the Bristol chapters and thus to include the 'passing of the veils')

Then come three grades peculiar to Baldwyn:

3 Knights of the Nine Elected Masters
4 Scots Knights Grand Architect (followed by the Royal Order of Scots Knights of Kilwinning, not itself one of the 'seven degrees')
5 Knights of the East, The Sword and the Eagle

Lastly, with rituals reserved to Baldwyn (and, in the case of the sixth, to the Percy Preceptory in Australia):

6 Knights of St John of Jerusalem, Palestine, Rhodes and Malta, and Knights Templar
7 Knights of the Rose Croix of Mount Carmel

Of the 6th it must be said that the one ceremony comprehends both knighthoods, that relating to Malta being the most prominent. Only the dress of a Knight Templar is worn by those present. Of the 7th, it is sufficient to observe that the candidate presents himself in the mantle of a Templar. It is a privilege indeed to be invited to witness the two workings although visitors to the Rose Croix chapter who are not in possession of the Templar and Malta degrees are asked to withdraw for a short period during the ceremony.

Daughters of Baldwyn

In the Charter of Compact of 1862 are listed six encampments which were said to have been warranted by Baldwyn during its period of independence. It was agreed that they would henceforth take precedence, among those already on the roll of Grand Conclave, according to the dates of their warrants. The six encampments thus provided for were

Antiquity, at Bath
Ascalon, at Birmingham
Holy Rood, at Warwick
Vale of Jehoshaphat, at Highbridge
Vale Royal, at Salisbury
Percy, at Adelaide, South Australia

The story of Antiquity is not quite as simple as this would suggest. It was, in fact, the one already working at Bath which Dunckerley took under his wing in 1791 and so was then 'time immemorial'. By 1810, however, it was in a sorry state and, despite a revival, became dormant until just before 1855 when Baldwyn granted a warrant for it. There are many reminders of that brief association with Baldwyn in the ritual which Antiquity practises today.

Ascalon was able to continue only until 1867, and Vale of Jehoshaphat and Vale Royal had ceased working before the charter was signed. Holy Rood presents an enigma because an erroneous date in an early *Liber Ordinis Templi* gives an impression that there were two encampments with this name – one under Grand Conclave and one created by Baldwyn. There was in fact only the one, established at Warwick in 1857 by Percy Wells of Baldwyn. During its life under Grand Conclave it met for a few years at Coventry but it then returned to Warwick in 1882 and soon after ceased to meet.

The continuing existence of Percy Preceptory in Australia has been mentioned elsewhere but deserves a place here to remind us that there is in the Southern Hemisphere the only undisputed offspring of Baldwyn to have survived and the only other preceptory in the world to have retained the privilege of using its ritual. In 1858, just four years before the end of independence, the same Percy Wells emigrated to Australia and there founded at Adelaide under a Baldwyn warrant an encampment bearing his Christian name. From 1862 to 1982 it bore the number 57 in the register of our Great Priory but is now at the head of that of the Great Priory of South Australia. What is especially interesting about Percy Preceptory is that, although in England *printed* rituals for the Baldwyn workings do not exist, in Adelaide they have – from 1948, if not earlier – used a neat little booklet based on a manuscript which had been sent out from Bristol by a Grand Superintendent.

Appendix F

THE ORDER OF ST. JOHN

The fuller title of 'The Grand Priory in the British Realm of the Most Venerable Order of the Hospital of St. John of Jerusalem' distinguishes this from the organizations, medieval and modern, masonic and non-masonic, regular and irregular, existing or ephemeral, which have been dealt with in this book. Although it has played no part in the history of our United Orders of the Temple and Malta, we have for many years recognized a relationship to it by directing our charity towards the St. John Ophthalmic Hospital at Jerusalem. This, in many senses, can be seen to be a spiritual ancestor of our two societies, perpetuating within a more specific field the services which the medieval Hospitallers initiated so long ago.

The members of the Order of St. John, which was 'revived' in 1831, look back to the Commanderies of the medieval Order, and in particular to those which, under various descriptions, were centred upon Clerkenwell in London, Kilmainham in Ireland and Torphichen in Scotland. For their stories, and for much more, the reader is enthusiastically referred to two books which are obtainable from St. John's Gate – the Order's headquarters at Clerkenwell: one is *A Short History of the Order of St. John,* by E. D. Renwick (1958), revised and continued by Major I. M. Williams through many more editions; the second, more comprehensive, is *The Knights of St. John in the British Realm,* by Colonel Sir Edwin King (1924), revised and continued by Sir Harry Luke. These splendidly illustrated volumes have been freely drawn upon for the information here provided.

The *langue* of the medieval Order in England was, in the early 1500s, flourishing under its Grand Prior, Sir Thomas Docwra (whose name is proudly borne by our preceptory at Hereford), but the dissolution in 1540 of the monasteries also brought to an end the

Hospitallers in England. A resuscitation under the Catholic Queen Mary I lasted only until Elizabeth came to the throne but, because Mary's 'letters patent' were never revoked, the Order of today regards the next 273 years as a period of suspended animation, thus allowing the events which culminated in 1831 to be regarded by them as a revival of the old rather than the birth of the new. From those early days, however, there survive the buildings at Clerkenwell which are the property of the present-day Order; in them many of the treasures of the past are displayed. Although the Priory Church was ruined by enemy action in 1941, the crypt – which was some eight centuries old – remained intact, and above it the church has been finely restored.

The resuscitation of the English *langue* was, surprisingly, given impetus in the 1820s by the French Capitular Commission having oversight of the reviving *langues* of Provence, Auvergne and France. They saw an English tongue as valuable support for themselves. In *AQC* 16 (1903) there is interesting reference to a jewel and a certificate, both illustrated, and a printed brief in French (text reproduced) of *L'Ordre Souverain de Saint-Jean de Jérusalem (Malte)*. These demonstrate the action taken in advance by a delegate from France to elect English members to the Order.

With the revival in 1831 was recognized the difficulty that the majority of the Christian citizens of England were now members of Protestant churches. The Order in this country would, therefore have to admit non-Catholics. The Sovereign Order of Malta in Rome at first accepted this situation but in 1858 withdrew its recognition. The English Order then had perforce to pursue its own course, which it did very effectively, but it would appear that a Catholic element stood apart for there is today in existence a 'Grand Priory of London of the Sovereign Order of St. John of Jerusalem'. This title suggests that it is independent of the papal Order of Malta in Rome, but there are indications of its Catholic membership.

Amid general rejoicing in 1963 a declaration of concord and co-operation healed the long-standing breach between the Sovereign Order of Malta and the English Order of St John and their common purpose was recognized.

A most valuable feature of the English Order's history has been the creation and development of the St. John Ambulance Brigade, and its spread to Scotland, Northern Ireland and throughout the Commonwealth. The Hospital at Jerusalem dates from 1882 when the Turkish Sultan granted land for it outside the Jaffa Gate.

The members of the masonic Order of Malta take pride in the fact that among the royal Grand Priors of the Order of St. John have been two of our own Grand Masters, Albert Edward, Prince of Wales (1888-1901) and the Duke of Connaught (1910-39). Many masonic knights have served and still serve at all levels of the Venerable Order of the Hospital of St. John of Jerusalem, and we all can and do support it in its splendid work.

Appendix G

RULERS, PATRONS AND ADMINISTRATORS

1 THE SUCCESSION OF GRAND MASTERS AND GREAT PRIORS

1791-1795 THOMAS DUNCKERLEY, Grand Master
Created Grand Conclave between January and June, and was installed as Grand Master on 24 June 1791 (*see* chapter 4). Died 10 November 1795
WILLIAM HANNAM, Acting Grand Master 10 November 1795 to 8 February 1796

1796-1800 THOMAS BOOTHBY PARKYNS, 1st LORD RANCLIFFE, Grand Master
Elected and installed on 3 February 1796. Died 17 November 1800
ROBERT GILL (Deputy Grand Master), Acting Grand Master 17 November 1800 to 11 March 1805

1800-1805 *Grand Conclave in abeyance (The Duke of Kent, Royal Grand Patron, granted a Charter in March 1804 to reconstitute Grand Conclave)*

1805-1807 H.R.H. EDWARD, DUKE OF KENT AND STRATHEARN (Royal Grand Patron), Grand Master
Elected 20 January 1805; resigned 12 April 1807

1807-1812 WALLER RODWELL WRIGHT, Grand Master
Elected and installed 12 April 1807; resigned 6 August 1812

1812-1843 H.R.H. AUGUSTUS FREDERICK, DUKE OF SUSSEX, Grand Master
Elected 3 May 1812; installed 6 August 1812; died 21 April 1843
JOHN CHRISTIAN BURCKHARDT (Grand Sub-Prior), Acting Grand Master 21 April 1843 to 3 April 1846

1846-1860 COLONEL CHARLES KEMEYS KEMEYS TYNTE, Grand Master
Elected 27 February 1846; installed 3 April 1846; died 22 November 1860
WILLIAM STUART, G.C.T. (Deputy Grand Master), Acting Grand Master 22 November 1860 to 10 May 1861

1861-1872 WILLIAM STUART, G.C.T., Grand Master
Elected 25 January 1861; installed 10 May 1861; resigned 13 December 1872
THE REVEREND JOHN HUYSHE, G.C.T. (Deputy Grand Master), Acting Grand Master 13 December 1872 to 7 April 1873

The Convent General was instituted on 13 December 1872 and can be deemed to have become operative when its Grand Master was installed on 7 April 1873

1872-1895 H.R.H. ALBERT EDWARD, PRINCE OF WALES, G.C.T.
Grand Master of the Convent General of England and Wales, and Ireland. Elected by England and Wales 13 December 1872; elected by Ireland 15 January 1873; installed 7 April 1873

1873-1876 **William Hale John Charles Pery, 3rd Earl of Limerick,** Great Prior of England and Wales
Appointed by patent dated 17 March 1873; installed 7 April 1873; resigned — September 1876

Colonel Shadwell Henry Clerke (Great Sub-Prior), Acting Great Prior of England and Wales — September 1876 to 8 December 1876

1876-1877 **Charles John Chetwynd Talbot, 19th Earl of Shrewsbury and 4th Earl of Talbot, G.C.T.,** Great Prior of England and Wales
Appointed by patent dated 7 December 1876; installed 8 December 1876; died 11 May 1877

Colonel Shadwell Henry Clerke (Great Sub-Prior), Acting Great Prior of England and Wales 11 May 1877 to 14 December 1877

1877-1896 **Edward Bootle Wilbraham, 2nd Lord Skelmersdale, G.C.T.** (*later* **Earl of Lathom),** Great Prior of England and Wales
Appointed by patent dated 25 October 1877; installed 14 December 1877

The Convent General was dissolved on 19 July 1895 and the Great Priory of England and Wales became a sovereign and independent authority

1895-1901 H.R.H. ALBERT EDWARD, PRINCE OF WALES, G.C.T. (Past Grand Master), SOVEREIGN OF THE UNITED ORDERS IN GREAT BRITAIN AND IRELAND, etc.

1896-1907 HENRY JAMES FITZROY, EARL OF EUSTON, G.C.T., Grand Master
Elected and installed 8 May 1896; resigned 13 December 1907

1907-1939 H.R.H. ARTHUR, DUKE OF CONNAUGHT AND STRATHEARN, Grand Master (Great Prior of Ireland, 1878-1895; Grand Master, Ireland, 1895-1942), and SOVEREIGN OF THE UNITED ORDERS IN GREAT BRITAIN AND IRELAND, etc.
Elected 13 December 1907; installed 8 May 1908; resigned 12 May 1939

1908-1912 Henry James Fitzroy, Earl of Euston, G.C.T. (Past Grand Master), Pro Grand Master
Installed 8 May 1908; died 10 May 1912

1912-1920 Richard Loveland Loveland, G.C.T., Pro Grand Master
Installed 20 September 1912; resigned 14 May 1920

1920-1932 Major-General Thomas Charles Pleydell Calley, G.C.T., Pro Grand Master
Installed 14 May 1920; died 14 February 1932

1932-1939 Henry George Charles Lascelles, 6th Earl of Harewood, G.C.T., Pro Grand Master
Installed as such 22 April 1932; elected Grand Master 12 May 1939

1939-1947 HENRY GEORGE CHARLES LASCELLES, 6th EARL OF HAREWOOD, G.C.T., Grand Master
Installed 12 May 1939; died 24 May 1947

GEORGE ST. VINCENT, 5th LORD HARRIS, G.C.T. (Great Seneschal), Acting Grand Master, 24 May 1947 to 12 December 1947

1947-1973 GEORGE ST VINCENT, 5th LORD HARRIS OF SERINGAPATAM AND MYSORE, G.C.T., Grand Master
Elected and installed 12 December 1947; resigned 16 May 1973

1973-1975 LIEUTENANT-COLONEL JOHN LEIGHTON BYRNE LEICESTER-WARREN, G.C.T., Grand Master
Elected and installed 16 May 1973; died 10 August 1975

HAROLD DEVEREUX STILL, G.C.T. (Great Seneschal), Acting Grand Master, 10 August 1975 to 19 May 1976

1976- HAROLD DEVEREUX STILL, G.C.T., Grand Master
Elected and installed 19 May 1976

2 PATRONS AND PAST GRAND MASTERS

1791-1805 H.R.H. PRINCE EDWARD (Duke of Kent, 1799).
1807-1820 Royal Grand Patron
1873-1901 H.M. QUEEN VICTORIA, Grand Patron
1901-1910 H.M. KING EDWARD VII (Past Grand Master), Patron
1937-1952 H.M. KING GEORGE VI, Past Grand Master

---

3 DEPUTY GRAND MASTERS, GREAT SUB-PRIORS OF THE TEMPLE AND GREAT SENESCHALS

GRAND CONCLAVE

Deputy Grand Masters

1796(?)-1807 ROBERT GILL
1807-1846 JOHN CHRISTIAN BURCKHARDT (Grand Sub-Prior *ad vitam* 1812-48)
1846-1861 WILLIAM STUART
1861-1872 THE REVEREND JOHN HUYSHE

CONVENT GENERAL

Great Sub-Priors

1873-1891 COLONEL SHADWELL HENRY CLERKE
1891-1895 HENRY JAMES FITZROY, EARL OF EUSTON

GREAT PRIORY

Great Seneschals

1896-1900 CHARLES SPENCER CANNING, VISCOUNT DUNGARVAN (*later* 10th Earl of Cork and Orrery)
1900-1905 EDWARD BOOTLE WILBRAHAM, 1st EARL OF LATHOM
1905-1912 RICHARD LOVELAND LOVELAND
1912-1931 COLONEL CHARLES WARREN NAPIER-CLAVERING
1932-1947 GEORGE ST. VINCENT, 5th LORD HARRIS
1947-1970 SIR ERIC STUDD
1971-1972 LIEUTENANT-COLONEL JOHN LEIGHTON BYRNE LEICESTER-WARREN
1973-1976 HAROLD DEVEREUX STILL
1976 JOHN HUSSEY HAMILTON VIVIAN, 4th LORD SWANSEA

4 GREAT VICE-CHANCELLORS

NOTE: Reference has been made in chapters 4 and 5 to John Gilbert who was Grand Scribe and Register in 1805 and to Robert Gill who served in the same office (under its varying designations) from 1805 until his death in 1822. In chapter 20 it was admitted that there had been difficulty in identifying the successors to Gill. Formal lists of the holders of Great office commence with 1873, at the inception of the Convent General.

1873-1893 WILLIAM TINKLER
1893-1896 MAJOR-GENERAL JOHN CROSLAND HAY
1896-1914 CHARLES FITZGERALD MATIER
1914-1923 ARTHUR DAVID HANSELL
1923-1955 MAJOR (SIR) THOMAS LUMLEY LUMLEY-SMITH
1955-1968 LIEUTENANT-COLONEL JOHN WALTER CHITTY
1968-1976 LIEUTENANT-COLONEL THE HON. MICHAEL EDWARDES
1976-1986 WILLIAM JOHNSTON LEAKE
1986 PETER GLYN WILLIAMS

---

5 GREAT PRIORS OF MALTA

1919-1931 LIEUTENANT-COLONEL JOHN MAURICE WINGFIELD
1931-1955 ARTHUR LIONEL FITZROY COOK
1956-1965 CECIL F. CUMBERLEGE
1965-1975 JOHN CHARLES HICKMAN TWALLIN
1975-1982 DR GILMORE LEONARD COLENSO COLENSO-JONES
1982- THOMAS WERE HOWARD

Appendix H

ROLL OF ENCAMPMENTS UNDER THE GRAND CONCLAVE IN 1809

extracted from the Statutes of that year

	Observance of Seven Degrees	London	T.I.	
	Redemption	York	T.I.	B
	Baldwin	Bristol	T.I.	
1	Trine	Bideford	1790	
2	Naval	Portsmouth	1791	2
3	St. John of Jerusalem	Redruth	1791	
4	Plains of Rama	Keighley	1792	3
5	Royal Edward	Bridgwater	1792	
6	Hope	Halifax	1793	4
7	Saint Bernard	Hollywood, Oldham	1793	
8	Bethlehem	Carlisle	1794	
9	Jerusalem	Manchester	1794?	5
10	Cross of Christ	London	1795	6
11	Ashton-under-Lyne	Ashton	1796	7
12	Boyne	Woolwich	1805	
13	Plains of Tabor	Colne	1805	
14	Plains of Brunswick	Haworth	1805	
15	Mount Carmel	London	1806	
16	Plains of Mamre	Haworth	1806	
17	Plains of Mamre	Burnley	1806	8
18	Union	Leeds	1806	
19	Saint Joseph	Middleton, Lancs.	1806	9
20	Royal Veteran	Plymouth	1806	10
21	Royal Edward	Stalybridge	1806	
22	Sinai	Hampton Court	1808	12

23	Saint Michael	Bury	1808	
24	Patriotic	Colchester	1808	
25	Concord	Harwich	1808	
26	Holy Cross	Whitehaven	1809	
27	Saint Salem	Stockport	1809	
28	Love and Friendship	Stockport	1809	14
29	Faith	Bradford	1809	13
30	Saint Patrick	Liverpool	1809	
31	Gethsemane	Bristol	1809	
32	True Friendship	Bristol	1809	
33	Mount Calvary	Coventry	1810 (8 Jan)	D

NOTES: 1 From the printed proceedings of Grand Conclave for 1807 it can be seen that certain of the Encampments listed above had previously been given other numbers.
2 In the right-hand column are given the present numbers of the preceptories which have survived to this day, not necessarily under the same names or in the same locations.

In the same edition of the *Statutes* is this 'List of Encampments discontinued, from not being able to assemble', the numbers being those allocated by Dunckerley:

	The Antiquity of Time Immemorial	Bath
1	Fortitude	formerly held in the First Dragoon Guards
4	Durnoverian *(sic)*	Dorchester
5	Harmony of Seven Degrees	Salisbury
6	Science of Seven Degrees	Salisbury
7	Holy Trinity	Hereford
12	Royal Edward of the Seven Degrees	Hampton Court Palace
14	Royal Gloucester	Southampton
15	Holy Sepulchre	Chichester

Appendix I

ENCAMPMENTS REMOVED FROM THE ROLL BEFORE THE ENUMERATION OF 1868

Trine	Bideford	1790	–
St. John of Jerusalem	Redruth	1791	–
Royal Edward	Bridgwater	1792	–
Saint Bernard	Oldham/Werneth	1793/1811	–
Bethlehem	Carlisle	1794	–
Boyne	Woolwich	1805	–
Plains of Brunswick	Haworth	1805	–
Fortitude	1st Dragoon Guards	Removed from roll prior to 1809. Dates of Const. unknown	
Durnovarian	Dorchester		
Harmony of Seven Degrees	Salisbury		
Science of Seven Degrees	Salisbury		
Holy Trinity	Hereford		
Royal Edward of the Seven Degrees	Hampton Court		
Royal Gloucester	Southampton		
Holy Sepulchre	Chichester		
Mount Carmel	London	1806	1867
Union	Leeds	1806	–
Sinai	Hampton Court	1808	–
Patriotic	Colchester	1808	–
Concord	Harwich	1808	–
Holy Cross	Whitehaven	1809	–
St. Patrick	Liverpool	1809	–
True Friendship	Bristol	1809	–
Gethsemane	Bristol/Cardiff	1809	–
Holy Trinity	Whitehaven	1811	1867
Joppa	Sunderland	1811	1865
La Réunion Désirée	Port-au-Prince, Haiti	1811	–
Trine	Portsea	prior to 1812	–
Mount Calvary	St. Kitts, W.I.		–

Frederick of Unity	London	1847	1867
Almeric de St. Maur[1]	Bolton	1853	1854
Ascalon[2]	Birmingham	–	1867
Vale of Jehoshaphat[3]	Highbridge	–	–
Vale Royal[3]	Salisbury	–	–
St. John	Simla	1860	1865
St. Michael and St. George	Corfu	1861	1865
Eastern Conclave of Redemption	Scinde	1866	1867

1 This encampment united in 1854 with that of St. Geoffrey de St. Omar, later No. 35; the warrant was surrendered in 1904.

2 Ascalon was one of the encampments warranted by Baldwyn at Bristol during its period of independence.

3 These encampments, also warranted by Baldwyn, were placed on the roll of Grand Conclave in 1862 when Baldwyn itself was restored. They had, however, already ceased to meet.

Appendix J

ROLL OF ENCAMPMENTS AND PRECEPTORIES

in the enumeration of 1868, since unchanged

T — allegiance transferred to another sovereign jurisdiction;
U — united with a more senior preceptory (indicated by its number)
E — erased from the register for other reasons

A	Abbey Chapter	Nottingham	T.I.	
B	Antient York Conclave of Redemption	York/Hull	T.I.	
C	Baldwyn	Bristol	T.I.	
D	Mount Calvary	Coventry/ Uxbridge/ London	T.I.	
E	Observance of the Seven Degrees	London	T.I.	E.1888
F	Union or Rougemont	Exeter	T.I.	
1	Antiquity	Bath	1791	
2	Royal Naval	Portsmouth	1791	
3	Plains of Rama	Keighley	1793	
4	Hope	Huddersfield	1793	
5	Jerusalem[1]	Manchester	1795	
6	St. George[2]	London	1795	
7	Loyal Volunteers	Ashton-under-Lyne	1796	
8	Plains of Mamre	Burnley	1806	
9	St. Joseph	Manchester	1806	
10	Royal Veterans'	Plymouth	1806	

11	[Neither a name nor any records can be traced for the preceptory which was allotted this number in 1868]			
12	St Michael	Bury/Rawtenstall	1808	
13	Faith	Bradford	1809	
14	Love and Friendship	Cheshire	1809	E.1894
15	St. Salem	Macclesfield	1808/1809	
16	Prudence	Ipswich	1811	
17	St. John of Jerusalem	Ulverston	1811	
18	Prince Edward	Todmorden	1811	
19	Trinity in Unity	Barnstaple	1812	
20	Royal Kent	Newcastle-on-Tyne	1812	
21	Salamanca	Halifax	1815/1860	
22	Hugh de Payens	Canada	1824	T.1875
23	Cornubian	Falmouth/Truro	1826	E.1888
24	Loyal Brunswick	Plymouth	1830	E.1927
25	Royal Sussex	Tiverton/Torquay	1834	
26	Faith and Fidelity	London	1838	
27	Sepulchre[3] (Sandeman Priory)	Calcutta/Ringwood	1840	
28	Stuart	Watford	1840	
29	Coeur de Lion	Oxford	1849	
30	Holy Cross	Axminster/Plymouth	1844	E.1893
31	All Souls'	Weymouth	1847	
32	Royal Gloucester	Southampton	1845	
33	St. James of Jerusalem	Bolton	1819/1849	
34	Albert	Ormskirk	1849	
35	United Preceptory of Almeric de St. Maur and Geoffrey de St. Omer	Manchester	1853	E.1940
36	Jacques de Molay	Liverpool	1850	
37	Melita[4]	Malta/Hertford	1815/1850	
38	Bermuda	Bermuda	1851/1890	
39	Fearnley	Dewsbury	1859	
40	Bladud	Bath	1852	
41	Faith	Wigan	1853	
42	Godefroi de Bouillon	Stoke-on-Trent	1853	
43	St. George's	Oldham	1854/1878	
44	Geoffrey de St. Aldemar	Canada	1854	T.1875
45	United Preceptory of Kemeys Tynte and Temple Cressing	London	1856	
46	William de la More the Martyr	Canada	1855	T.1875
47	Godefroi de Bouillon	Canada	1855	T.1875

48	Keymeys Tynte	London	1856	U.1893 (45)
49	William de la More	St. Helens	1856	
50	Tynte	Taunton	1857	E.1870
51	Pembroke of Australasia	Melbourne	1857	T.1982
52	Richard de Vernon	Dudley	1857	
53	St. Augustine	Lahore	1857	E.1975
54	Richard Coeur de Lion	Canada	1857	T.1875
55	Holy Rood (Baldwyn warrant)	Warwick/ Coventry	1857	E.1894
56	Hugh de Payens	Blackburn	1857	
57	Percy (Baldwyn warrant)	Adelaide	1858	T.1982
58	Nova Scotia[5]	Canada	1858	T.1875
59	Mount Zion	Bombay	1859	E.1888
60	Calpe	Gibraltar	1859	
61	Edmund Plantagenet	Warrington	1859	
62	Jacques de Molay	Australia	1859	E.1888
63	Ascalon	Poona	1859	E.1899
64	Excelsior	21st Ft.	1860	E.1886
65	Royal Kent	Calcutta	1861	E.1887
66	De Furnival	Sheffield	1861 ·	
67	Howe-Beauceant	Birmingham	1850/1894	
68	St. Amand	Worcester	1861	
69	Cabbell	Norwich	1862	
70	Union	Guyana	1862	
71	Celestial	Shanghai	1862	E.1900
72	Coteswold of St. Augustin	Cheltenham	1863	
73	Coromandel[6]	Madras/ Bangalore/ Wellington	1828	
74	Harcourt	Richmond	1863	E.1890
75	Coeur de Lion	Canada	1863	T.1875
76A	William Stuart	Aldershot	1864	
76B	Royal Edward	Stalybridge	1806	
77	Star of the West	Barbados	1864	
78	Victoria	Hong Kong	1864	
79	Wulfruna	Wolverhampton	1864	
80	Royal Plantagenet	Great Yarmouth	1864	
81	Loyal Burmah	Rangoon	1865	E.1902
82	Hinxman	Brisbane	1865	E.1894
83	Grove	Ewell	1865	E.1888
84	Invicta	Chatham	1865	E.1869
85	Star of the East	Singapore	1866	E.1897
86	Royal Deccan	Secunderabad	1866/1897	E.1918
87	Southern Cross	Cape Town	1866	E.1888
88	Plantagenet	Canada	1866	T.1875

89	Plains of Mamre	Haworth	1806/1867	
90	Restormel (St. Andrew Priory)	Hayle	1867	
91	Geoffroy de Bouillon	Birkenhead	1867	
92	Palestine	Swansea	1867	E.1888
93	Mount Calvary	Bombay	1867	E.1888
94	Mount Moriah	Scinde	1867	E.1888
95	De Lacy	Southport	1867	
96	Plantagenet/Sussex	Canada	1867	T.1875
97	Prince of Peace	Preston	1867	
98	Hyde	Poole	1867	
99	Ceylon	Colombo/Kandy	1867	
100	De Tabley	Knutsford	1868	
101	Ancient Ebor	York	1868	
102	Tancred	Cambridge	1868	
103	Hurontario	Canada	1869	T.1875
104	Union de Molay	Canada	1869	T.1875
105	Beauceant	Birmingham	1850	U.189-4 (67)
106	King Baldwin	Canada	1861	T.1875
107	St. George	Australia	1869	E.1888
108	Mount Calvary	Canada	1870	T.1875
109	Moore	Canada	1870	T.1875
110	Plains of Tabor	Colne	1805	
111	Observance	Madras	1853	E.1888
112	Mount Lebanon	Bombay	1871	E.1888
113	Harington	Canada	1871	T.1875
114	Fidelity	Leeds	1871	
115	Gwent	Newport	1871	
116	St. John the Almoner	Canada	1872	T.1875
117	New Temple	London	1872	
118	Mount Grace	Hartlepool	1872	
119	Gondemar	Canada	1872	T.1875
120	Ode de St. Amand	Canada	1872	T.1875
121	Worlebury of St. Dunstan	Bury	1872	
122	Palestine	Canada	1872	T.1875
123	St. Bernard[7]	Bury	1872	
124	Royal Mysore Excelsior	Bangalore	1872	E.1907
125	Sussex (Southdown Priory)	Eastbourne	1872	
126	De Warenne	Brighton	1873	
127	Bard of Avon	Hampton Court/ London	1873	
128	Oxford, Cambridge and United[8]	London	1873	
129	Holy Palestine	London	1874	E.1916
130	St. Bernard de Clairvaux	Canada	1874	T.1875

131	Holy Sanctuary	London	1875	
132	Grosvenor	Chester	1875	
133	Diamond in the Desert	Kimberley	1875	
134	Blondel	London	1877	E.1884
135	Bosbury	London	1877	E.1888
136	Mount Carmel	Palumpore	1877	E.1888
137	Himalaya/Duke of Connaught and Strathearn's Himalaya[9]	Simla/Ambala/ Worthing	1877	
138	Acre	Allahabad	1877	E.1889
139	St. Cuthbert's	Darlington	1878	
140	Studholme	London	1878	
141	Ardvorlich	Rawalpindi	1878	E.1899
142	Royal Canterbury	Christchurch, N.Z.	1878	E.1894
143	Temple Bruer	Lincoln	1879	
144	Tyrawley	Tasmania	1879	E.1894
145	Egbert	Winchester	1879	E.1894
146	Black Prince	Canterbury	1880	
147	Jamaica	Jamaica	1880	E.1894
148	Natalia	Pieter-maritzburg	1880	
149	Royds	Morecambe	1880	
150	Plantagenet	Timaru, N.Z.	1882	E.1894
151	Vasco de Gama (Holy Sepulchre Priory)	Port Elizabeth	1883	
152	Rothley Temple	Leicester	1884	
153	(Duke of) Connaught and Strathearn	Delhi/Meerut	1884	U.1931 (137)
154	Shadwell Clerke	London	1884	
155	Lullingstone	London	1885	
156	Victoria Jubilee	Durban	1886	
157	Rose of Lancaster	Blackpool	1887	
158	Amphibious	Heckmondwike	1892	
159	Peveril	Derby	1893	
160	Johannesburg	Johannesburg	1893	
161	Robert de Sable	Carlisle	1893	
162	Temple Court	Guildford	1894	
163	Ascalon[10]	London	1894	
164	Colombo	Sri Lanka	1895	
165	St. Michael	London	1895	E.1952
166	St. George in Burma	Moulmein	1896	E.1923
167	Westralia	Perth, W.A.	1897	T.1984
168	Mount Zion	South Africa	1897/1931	
169	Earl of Euston	Adelaide	1898	T.1982
170	Bernard de Tremelay	Walsall	1899	

171	Duke of Albany	Brisbane	1900	T.1985
172	Connaught/Connaught Army and Navy	Aldershot/ London	1901	
173	King Edward VII	London	1902	
174	Holy Sepulchre	St. Leonards	1902	
175	Australasian[11]	Melbourne	1902	U.---- (51)
176	Metropolitan[11]	Melbourne	1902	T.1982
177	Ardvorlich[12]	Rawalpindi	1903	E.1922
178	Empress	London	1903	
179	Holy Rood	Cambridge	1904	
180	Broken Hill	New South Wales	1904	T.1984
181	Royal Kent	Calcutta	1905	U.196-2 (27)
182	Iles	Rangoon	???	E.1976
183	Sancta Maria	London	1906	
184	St. Hilary	Birkenhead	1906	
185	Galilee	London	1907	
186	Sydney	N.S.W.	1907	T.1984
187	Erimus	Saltburn	1908	
188	Baluchistan	Quetta/London	1908	
189	Jamaica	Kingston	1909	
190	Sutcliffe	Grimsby	1910	
191	San Martin	Buenos Aires	1911	
192	Royal George	Jamaica	1911	E.1922
193	Saint Chad	Shrewsbury	1911	
194	Loveland	Boscombe	1911	
195	Shanghai	Shanghai/ Hong Kong	1911	
196	Croydon	Croydon	1912	
197	St. Thomas	Bombay	1912	E.1966
198	Santa Rosa	Buenos Aires	1913	E.1985
199	King George V	Keighley/Leeds	1913	
200	Morganwg	Cardiff	1913	
201	St. Richard	Chichester	1914	
202	Londesborough	Bridlington	1917	
203	Sir George Somers	Bermuda	1918	
204	Wellesley	Sindlesham	1918	
205	Integrity	Morley	1918	
206	Annus Mirabilis	London	1918	
207	Victory	Northampton	1918	
208	Thornton	Brighton	1919	
209	Public Schools	London	1919	
210	Pax	Widnes	1919	
211	King Ina	Taunton	1919	
212	Richard Coeur de Lion	King's Heath	1920	

213	De Ros	Harrogate	1920	
214	Chantry	Wakefield	1920	
215	Geraldton	W. Australia	1920	T.1984
216	Wharfedale	Otley	1920	
217	Palestine	Wallasey	1920	
218	Perseverance	Kettering	1921	
219	Golden Square	London	1921	
220	North Queensland	Townsville	1921	T.1985
221	Avery	Seaforth, N.S.W.	1922	T.1984
222	Finchale	Sunderland	1922	
223	Humber	Hull	1922	
224	Roffa's Camp	Rochester	1922	
225	Kyngstun	Surbiton	1923	
226	Lindisfarne	Berwick	1923	
227	Eagle of Taxila	Murree/ Rawalpindi	1923	E.1972
228	Ballarat	Australia	1924	T.1982
229	Peter de Erdington	Sutton Coldfield	1924	
230	Airedale	Baildon	1924	
231	Menai	Rhyl	1924	
232	Chibburn	Whitley Bay	1924	
233	Haliwerfolc	Durham	1924	
234	de l'Isle Adam	Chester	1924	
235	Temple	Halifax	1925	
236	Wendlynburgh	Wellingborough	1925	
237	Vectis	Ryde, I.O.W.	1925	
238	Scardeburg	Scarborough	1925	
239	Brandling	Gosforth	1925	
240	United Priors	Huntingdon	1925	
241	Beauceant	Queensland	1926	T.1985
242	Carpentaria	Queensland	1926	T.1985
243	St. Oswald	Peterborough	1927	
244	Selwood of St. John	Frome	1927	
245	Earl of Stradbroke	Melbourne	1927	T.1982
246	Royal Canterbury	Christchurch, N.Z.	1927	T.1984
247	Geelong	Victoria	1927	T.1982
248	Capricorn	Queensland	1928	T.1985
249	Riverina	Wagga Wagga	1928	T.1984
250	Star of the Valley	Victoria	1928	T.1982
251	Sydenham	London	1928	
252	Ivalda	Victoria	1928	T.1982
253	Staines	Staines	1928	
254	Waitemata	Auckland	1928	T.1984
255	Burwell	W. Australia	1928	T.1984

256	Maplestead	Colchester	1928	
257	Crystal Palace	London	1928	
258	Crusaders	Maidenhead	1929	
259	Trafalgar	Batley	1929	
260	Ampthill	Bedford	1929	
261	De Mandeville	Chingford	1929	
262	Werrigar	Victoria	1929	T.1982
263	Western	Victoria	1930	T.1982
264	Cressing	Gerrards Cross/ Henley	1930	
265	Grey Friars	Doncaster	1930	
266	Saint Alban	St. Albans	1930	
267	Vexillum Belli	Brisbane	1930	T.1985
268	Herga	Harrow	1930	
269	Temple Chelsin	Hertford	1931	
270	Bloemfontein	South Africa	1931	
271	St. Chad's	London/ Chingford	1932	
272	Love and Friendship	Stockport	1933	
273	Keystone	Transvaal	1934	
274	Chelmersforde	Chelmsford	1934	
275	St. Lawrence	South Shields	1934	
276	Mackay	Queensland	1935/1961	T.1985
277	Star of the East	Singapore	1935	
278	Temple	King's Heath	1936	
279	Wide Bay	Queensland	1936	T.1985
280	St. Helier	Jersey	1936	
281	St. John the Evangelist	High Barnet	1936	
282	Britannic of Madeira	London	1936	
283	Temple Dinsley	Letchworth	1937	
284	Brinkburn	Morpeth	1937	
285	St. George	Auckland	1938	T.1984
286	Bromley	Penge	1938	
287	Royal Taranaki	Taranaki, N.Z.	1938	T.1984
288	Kosmos	Johannesburg	1939	
289	Transvaal	Pretoria	1940	
290	Golden Cheronese	Kuala Lumpur	1941	
291	Aotea	Taranaki, N.Z.	1942	T.1984
292	Wycliffe	Darlington	1942	
293	Holy Rood	Warwick	1942	
294	Ivanhoe	Leicester	1944	
295	St. Katharine's	Southend	1944	
296	St. Thomas	Stockport	1944	E.1967
297	Talpioth	W. Australia	1944	T.1984
298	Saint Laurence	Pudsey	1944	
299	Newcastle	Newcastle, N.S.W.	1945	T.1984

300	Military Lodges'	London	1945	
301	Heneage	Grantham	1946	
302	Athlit	W. Australia	1946	T.1984
303	Golden Cross	Kalgoorlie	1946	T.1984
304	Chertsey	Chertsey	1946	
305	St. John's	Victoria	1946	T.1982
306	Narrogin	W. Australia	1946	T.1984
307	Joppa	W. Australia	1947	T.1984
308	Dukinfield	Dukinfield	1947	
309	Pymmes Park	Chingford	1947	
310	Hubert-de-Burgh	Southend	1947	
311	Sanctuary	W. Australia	1947	T.1984
312	Wordsworth	Calcutta	1947	U.1962 (27)
313	Edmund Grindal	Whitehaven	1947	
314	St. Hugh	Banbury	1947	
315	John F. Cleeves	Cheshunt	1947	
316	Tees	Stockton	1947	
317	St. Swithin	N.S.W.	1948	T.1984
318	St. George	Stockport	1948	
319	Giraldus Cambrensis	Llanelli	1948	
320	All Saints'	Gainsborough	1948	
321	Royal Colonial Institute	London	1948	
322	William Longspee	Salisbury	1948	
323	Beaumont	Oxford	1948	
324	St. Paul	Bradford	1948	
325	Temple Ewell	Dover	1948	
326	Faith	Sale	1949	
327	Temple	Sandbach	1949	
328	Fellowship	S. Australia	1949	T.1982
329	Albury	N.S.W.	1949	T.1984
330	Lynn Regis	King's Lynn	1950	
331	Holy Trinity	Coventry	1950	
332	Holy Cross	Stechford	1951	
333	St. Vincent	Tunbridge Wells	1951	
334	Northern Transvaal	S. Africa	1951	
335	St. Michael	N.S.W.	1951	T.1984
336	Port Adelaide	S. Australia	1952	T.1982
337	St. Paul's	N.S.W.	1952	T.1984
338	St. Saviour's	Sutton	1953	
339	De Umfraville	Gateshead	1954	
340	Temple Balsall	Temple Balsall	1954	
341	King Richard I	Bristol	1954	
342	Tuarangi	Ashburton, N.Z.	1955	T.1984
343	Chaffey	Victoria	1955	T.1982
344	Ringwood	Victoria	1955	T.1982

345	Victoria Centenary	Victoria	1955	T.1982
346	Talisman	W. Australia	1955	T.1984
347	Rhodes	Bulawayo	1955	
348	Abbeydale	Dore	1956	
349	Carmelite	Boston	1956	
350	Roan Antelope[13]	Zambia	1956	
351	Duke of Sussex	W. Australia	1956	T.1984
352	Armadale	W. Australia	1956	T.1984
353	Amuri	Amberley, N.Z.	1956	T.1984
354	Estune Command	Nailsea	1957	
355	Aurora	St. Andrew's, N.Z.	1957	T.1984
356	Crusader	W. Australia	1958	T.1984
357	Pilgrim	Portsmouth	1958	
358	Ascension	W. Australia	1958	T.1984
359	Lakemba	W. Australia	1958	T.1984
360	Gascoigne	Croydon	1958	
361	Ascalon	Rugby	1958	
362	Tamworth	N.S.W.	1959	T.1984
363	St. John	Auckland	1959	T.1984
364	St. George at Stoneleigh	Surbiton	1959	
365	Dean Forest of St. Mary	Newnham	1959	
366	Illawarra St. George	N.S.W.	1960	T.1984
367	St. Mary and All Saints'	Stourport	1960	
368	Agnus Dei	N.S.W.	1960	T.1984
369	Sir John Kent	Stafford	1960	
370	Le Crac des Chevaliers	Harare	1960	
371	West Kent	Bromley	1961	
372	Cooroora	Queensland	1961	T.1985
373	Axtane of St. John Jerusalem	Wrotham	1961	
374	St. John Canberra	Canberra	1961	T.1984
375	Bendigo	Victoria	1961	T.1982
376	Sir Thomas Docwra	Hereford	1961	
377	Port Pirie	S. Australia	1961	T.1982
378	St. John at Stoneleigh	Surbiton	1962	
379	St. Peter and St. Paul	Marlborough	1962	
380	Burnett	Queensland	1963	T.1985
381	Royal	Filey	1963	
382	Felix E. Crate	Upminster	1963	
383	Joseph Moffett	Berkhamsted	1963	
384	De Conlay	Queensland	1963	T.1985
385	St. John of Beverley	Beverley	1963	
386	Wongan Hills	W. Australia	1963	T.1984
387	Central Highlands	Queensland	1963	T.1985
388	Twickenham	Twickenham	1963	

389	Aylesbury	Aylesbury	1964	
390	Craven	Skipton	1964	
391	Holy Trinity	Gravesend	1964	
392	Pilgrims Way	Wilmington	1964	
393	Alpha	Brisbane	1964	T.1985
394	Uxbridge	Uxbridge	1964	
395	Wynkbourne	Mansfield	1964	
396	St. John the Baptist	Bromsgrove	1964	
397	Dandenong St. Paul's	Victoria	1965	T.1982
398	Saint Clement	West Bromwich	1965	
399	St. Laurence	Long Eaton	1965	
400	Crux Christi	Horsham	1965	
401	Thanet	Margate	1966	
402	Boxley Abbey	Maidstone	1966	
403	Anchor	Northallerton	1966	
404	St. Alkmund	Whitchurch	1966	
405	St. Andrew's	Durban	1966	
406	Stroud of St. Michael	Stroud	1966	
407	Roger de Clinton	Wolverhampton	1966	
408	Hales Abbey	Stourbridge	1967	
409	Charles Herbert Perram	Luton/Radlett	1967	
410	Sir John Babington	Loughborough	1968	
411	Robert de Stafford	Stoke-on-Trent	1968	
412	Crux Meridionalis	Sao Paulo	1968	
413	Pelham	Worksop	1969	
414	Simon de Montford	Evesham	1969	
415	Candia	Nottingham	1969	
416	Royston	Royston	1969	
417	Olivier-de-la-Marche	Leiden	1969	
418	St. John	Diss	1969	
419	Far West	Transvaal	1969	
420	Ulverscroft	Leicester	1969	
421	Bernard de Frankley	Northfield	1969	
422	St. Andrew's in Gippsland	Victoria	1970	T.1982
423	Bertram de Verdun	Burton	1970	
424	Hatfield	Radlett	1970	
425	Sacryham	Caterham	1970	
426	Whyalla	S. Australia	1970	T.1982
427	Menevia	Aberaeron	1970	
428	Maples	Manchester	1970	
429	Southgate	Southgate	1970	
430	Sir Oliver Starkey	Slough	1970	
431	Powys	Telford	1971	
432	St. Michael and St. Mary	Basingstoke	1971	
433	Westwood	Bexleyheath	1971	
434	Arthur Dentith	Saffron Walden	1971	

435	Tamehana	Matamata, N.Z.	1971	T.1984
436	St. Michael's	Sittingbourne	1971	
437	Melbourne	Victoria	1972	T.1982
438	Robert Loyd	Henley	1972	
439	Hereward the Wake	March	1972	
440	Earl of Lathom	Liverpool	1972	
441	Essex	Southend	1972	
442	Sir Peter de Tany	Harlow	1972	
443	Clermont	Nottingham	1972	
444	Rougemont	Durban	1973	
445	Rockingham	W. Australia	1973	T.1984
446	Emmaus	Surbiton	1973	
447	Whyte Stone	Farnham	1973	
448	Edgbaston	Birmingham	1974	
449	Gauntlet	Harrow	1974	
450	All Hallows	Twickenham	1974	
451	Walter Short	Thetford	1974	
452	Salebeia	Selby	1974	
453	St. Thomas a Becket	Ilford	1974	
454	St. David	Connah's Quay	1974	
455	Keynsham of St. Kenya	Keynsham	1975	
456	Royal Victoria	Bahamas	1975	
457	Sir Robert Mavesyn	Rugeley	1975	
458	Warwickshire	Warwick	1975	
459	Swan	W. Australia	1975	T.1984
460	Park Lane	Johannesburg	1975	
461	St. Wilfrid of Hexham	Hexham	1975	
462	Corpus Christi	Bridgford	1975	
463	Macleod	Hertford	1975	
464	Cygnet	Amersham	1975	
465	Ralph Le Strange	Bridgnorth	1975	
466	St. Paul's	Skegness	1975	
467	Hugo de Payens	Wickford	1975	
468	Trinity	S. Australia	1976	T.1982
469	St. Aidan	Amble	1976	
470	Holy Cross	Uckfield	1976	
471	Concordia	Transvaal	1976	
472	St. John the Baptist	S. Australia	1976	T.1982
473	High Peak	New Mills	1976	
474	Outremer	Newbury	1976	
475	Lord Harris	Ashford	1976	
476	Cumba	Yeovil	1976	
477	Bright Morning Star	Brighton	1976	
478	Stephen Langton	Dorking	1976	
479	Strathmore	Burnopfield	1976	
480	Launceston Castle	Launceston	1977	

481	St. Oswald	Newcastle-on-Tyne	1977	
482	Trinity	Stechford	1977	
483	Castle Hill	N.S.W.	1977	T.1984
484	Frederick Friday	Canterbury	1977	
485	Lanfranc	Harrow	1977	
486	St. George's	Brida, Netherlands	1978	
487	Terra Sancta	Chipping Norton	1978	
488	William of Normandy	Battle	1978	
489	Essex Jubilee	Wickford	1979	
490	West Australia Jubilee	W. Australia	1979	T.1984
491	St. George of Guernsey	St. Peter Port	1979	
492	St. Aldhelm	Malmesbury	1979	
493	Corinium of St. John the Baptist	Cirencester	1979	
494	de ffaryngton	Leyland	1979	
495	Pilgrim	Newark	1980	
496	St. Osyth	Clacton	1980	
497	Walsingham	Fakenham	1980	
498	Saint German's of Mann	Peel, I.O.M.	1980	
499	Robert de Turnham	Bletchley	1980	
500	Shirley Woolmer	Sidcup	1981	
501	Avon of St. Andrew	Avonmouth	1981	
502	Holy Palestine	Swansea	1981	
503	St. Bernard de Clairvaux	Spui Terneuzen	1981	
504	St. Peter's	Leiden	1981	
505	St. Maarten's	Groningen	1981	
506	Gloucester of St. Nicholas	Gloucester	1981	
507	Waltham Holy Cross	Chingford	1981	
508	Lily of the Dale	Victoria	1981	T.1982
509	Acre	Natal	1981	
510	Nottinghamshire	Nottingham	1981	
511	Phoenix	Simonstown, S. Africa	1981	
512	Guild of Freemen	London	1981	
513	Norman Wright	Stamford	1981	
514	Friendship and Care	Sindlesham	1981	
515	Robert de Bruys	Keswick	1982	
516	Northern Territory	Darwin	1982	
517	Agincourt	Camberley	1982	
518	Middleseaxe	Uxbridge	1982	
519	King John	Worcester	1982	
520	Round Table	Chesterfield	1983	
521	Alpha	Finland	1983	T.1985
522	Prior's Haven	N. Shields	1983	

523	Stydd	Belper	1983	
524	Ranulph de Blundeville	Leek	1983	
525	St. George of Throckley	Throckley	1984	
526	Beta	Finland	1984	T.1985
527	Gamma	Finland	1984	T.1985
528	Omega	Johannesburg	1984	
529	St. Alphege	Solihull	1984	
530	William de Ferrars	Burton-on-Trent	1984	
531	St. Stephen	Redditch	1984	
532	Rio de Janeiro	Brazil	1985	
533	Toison d'Or	Zaandam	1985	
534	Lord Roberts	Somerset W., S. Africa	1985	
535	Coeur de Lion	Dundee, S. Africa	1985	
536	Coeur de Lion	Johannesburg	1985	
537	Wudcestre	Ashington	1985	
538	Dunwich	Southwold	1986	
539	[The preceptory which would have borne this number was not consecrated]			
540	St. Michael	Bilthoren	1986	
541	Abbey	Nuneaton	1987	
542	St. George	George, S. Africa	1987	
543	Harold Devereux Still	Radlett	1987	
544	Martyn	Sudbury	1987	
545	Staffordshire and Shropshire	Wolverhampton	1987	
546	John O'Gaunt	Newcastle-under-Lyme	1987	
547	Owain Glyndwr of Installed Preceptors	Llanelli	1987	
548	Taciturnus	Rotterdam	1987	
549	Worcestershire	Worcester	1988	
550	Marmaduke Lumley	Chester-le-Street	1988	
551	King Arthur of Avalon	Glastonbury	1988	
552	Kent Body Guard	Gravesend	1989	
553	Wolds	Louth	1989	
554	Holy Cross	Daventry	1989	
555	Oakley	Bromley	1989	
556	Sant Madoc	Porthcawl	1989	
557	Kingsbury	Dunstable	1990	
558	Northwich	Northwich	1990	

[1] This preceptory had originally been warranted by the Grand Lodge of All England at York on 10 October 1786. It was given a Grand Conclave charter on 20 May 1795.

[2] Until 1857 this was known as the Cross of Christ Encampment.

[3] In 1962, Royal Kent Preceptory No 181 and Wordsworth Preceptory No. 312, both of Calcutta, were amalgamated with No. 27

[4] From 1979 to 1983 the Melita Preceptory was renamed Mediterranean.

[5] This was first chartered in 1839 as St. John's by the Royal Grand Conclave of Scotland.

[6] From 1863 to 1916 known as St. John of Jerusalem (with Pitt McDonald Priory of Malta).

[7] Until about 1903 this preceptory was known as Allpass.

[8] From 1873 to 1919 it was known as the Oxford and Cambridge University Preceptory.

[9] The Duke of Connaught and Strathearn Preceptory No. 153 united with the Himalaya Preceptory No 137 in 1931.

[10] Until 1911 this was known as the Camden Preceptory.

[11] These two preceptories had been warranted some years before by the Great Priory of Canada and in 1900 had taken part in the formation of an irregular Sovereign Grand Priory of Victoria. That having been dissolved by mutual consent, the two preceptories were in 1902 granted English warrants. Some time before 1916, Australasian Preceptory united with Pembroke Preceptory No 51.

[12] It is improbable that this preceptory was ever consecrated.

[13] Originally named Coeur de Lion. The change was effected in 1978.

INDEX

compiled by Frederick Smyth
Member of the Society of Indexers

If not otherwise qualified, all references may be taken to be to the English Constitutions of the United Orders, the Craft, the Royal Arch, etc.

A preceptory still in existence is usually indexed under its modern name and number, with a cross-reference where appropriate to the encampment from which it derived.

Masonic abbreviations used include: GM – Grand Master (of Great Priories and the jurisdictions from which they developed. If the Grand Mastership is of the Craft or another Order, this is shown); GMM – Grand Master Mason of the Craft, Scotland; ProGM and DepGM are self evident; Gt – Great; IC and SC denote the Irish and Scottish Constitutions respectively; A&AR – Ancient and Accepted Rite. 'KT' is used occasionally to mean 'the Order of the Temple'.

The more important page references are printed in **bold** type; plate numbers are in *italic*, and in many instances it will be the caption rather than the illustration itself to which the reader is being directed.